Praise for
SUPER SCRATCH
PROGRAMMING ADVENTURE!

"Reveals the power of this deceptively simple programming language. . .
A fun way to learn how to program Scratch, even for adults."
—Mark Frauenfelder, Boing Boing

"A great introduction to game design. Kids will start building games
from the first page."
—Liz Upton, The Raspberry Pi Project

"If you think you might have a future programmer on your hands,
it's time to introduce your kid to Scratch. . . . *Super Scratch Programming Adventure!* makes it even easier to get started."
—Ruth Suehle, *GeekMom*

"If you have a kid who plays around with a computer and can read
even a little, get this."
—Greg Laden, *National Geographic*'s *ScienceBlogs*

"An enjoyable and highly accessible introduction to this technology
and the power of computing."
—Patrice Gans, *Education Week*'s *BookMarks*

"If you've got a child or maybe even a classroom of students who are
wanting to make their own games, Scratch is a great option. . . . For
structured training that is also entertaining, *Super Scratch Programming Adventure!* will make a great textbook."
—James Floyd Kelly, *GeekDad*

"Walks readers through a series of extremely well-designed game-design
projects, each of which introduces a new concept or two to young programmers, providing a gentle learning curve for mastering Scratch's
many powerful features."
—Cory Doctorow, Boing Boing

"If you're looking for a way to get your kid interested in programming,
and Scratch in particular, I can't recommend this Scratch book enough."
—Chris O'Brien, *San Jose Mercury News*' *SiliconBeat*

SUPER SCRATCH
PROGRAMMING ADVENTURE!

LEARN TO PROGRAM BY MAKING COOL GAMES!

THE LEAD PROJECT

no starch press

Printed in USA

First printing

17 16 15 14 13   1 2 3 4 5 6 7 8 9

ISBN-10: 1-59327-531-5
ISBN-13: 978-1-59327-531-0

Publisher: William Pollock
Adviser: Dr. Rosanna Wong Yick-ming, DBE, JP
Editorial Team: Yolanda Chiu, Alice Lui, Edmond Kim Ping Hui
Contributors: Edmond Kim Ping Hui (Book Contents); Man Chun Chow, Chun Hei Tse,
    Vincent Wong (Assistance & Photography)
Interior Design: LOL Design Ltd.
Production Editor: Serena Yang
Cover Design: Tina Salameh
Developmental Editor: Tyler Ortman
Technical Reviewer: Michael Smith-Welch
Compositors: Laurel Chun and Riley Hoffman
Proofreader: Alison Law

For information on distribution, translations, or bulk sales,
please contact No Starch Press, Inc. directly:

No Starch Press, Inc.
245 8th Street, San Francisco, CA 94103
phone: 415.863.9900; fax: 415.863.9950; info@nostarch.com; http://www.nostarch.com/

CONTENTS

Let's get to know Scratch! We'll also learn about sprites
and coordinates.

This is where you'll make your the first game. You'll also
learn how to create new costumes and program a sprite's
movements, reactions, and sound effects.

While writing this two-part game, you'll learn how to
control the flow of a Scratch project. You'll see how to
keep score using variables and control the order of the
game using broadcasts.

You'll learn to control sprites with the mouse, program
objects to bounce back, and more.

You'll program a soccer game with a targeting system,
several related rules, interactive sound effects, and a
vivid, animated background!

FOREWORD

Scratch is more than a piece of software. It is part of a broader educational mission. We designed Scratch to help young people prepare for life in today's fast-changing society. As young people create Scratch projects, they are not just learning how to write computer programs. They are learning to think creatively, reason systematically, and work collaboratively—essential skills for success and happiness in today's world.

It has been exciting to see all of the creative ways that young people are using Scratch. On the Scratch website (*http://scratch .mit.edu/*), young people from around the world are sharing a wide variety of creative projects: animated stories, adventure games, interactive tutorials, guided tours, science experiments, online newsletters, and much more. Scratch is a digital sandbox where young people can express themselves creatively—and, in the process, develop as creative thinkers.

Super Scratch Programming Adventure! will help introduce more young people to the creative possibilities of Scratch. The book grows out of one of the world's most innovative and productive Scratch initiatives, organized by the Hong Kong Federation of Youth Groups. I'm delighted that their ideas and activities are now available to teachers, parents, and children around the world.

As you read this book, let your imagination run wild. What will you create with Scratch?

Enjoy the adventure!

Mitchel Resnick

Professor Mitchel Resnick
Director, MIT Scratch Team
MIT Media Lab

A NOTE OF THANKS

The Hong Kong Federation of Youth Groups created the Learning through Engineering, Art and Design (LEAD) Project in 2005 in collaboration with the MIT Media Lab and the Chinese University of Hong Kong. The LEAD Project promotes hands-on, design-based activities with the creative use of technology and aims to develop an innovative spirit among the youth of Hong Kong. Since its founding, it has promoted technology education on a grand scale, reaching more than 1,000,000 students, parents, and educators.

Super Scratch Programming Adventure! is our second of three books about Scratch and the first to be translated into English. This book highlights the playful spirit of learning to program with Scratch, which inspires young people to apply digital technologies in imaginative and innovative ways.

We are very grateful to the MIT Media Lab, which has been our partner since LEAD was established in 2005. We are particularly appreciative of Professor Mitchel Resnick and Mr. Michael Smith-Welch, who have always been LEAD's staunchest supporters and greatest cheerleaders. Because of their unwavering belief in Scratch and in LEAD, you are now able to read this English edition.

We hope this book inspires you to design your very own games, projects, and more with Scratch.

Dr. Rosanna Wong Yick-ming, DBE, JP
Executive Director
The Hong Kong Federation of Youth Groups

A NOTE FOR PARENTS AND EDUCATORS

Scratch opens up an exciting world of computer programming for kids and other beginning programmers. To follow along with this book and use Scratch 2.0, you'll need:

- A computer with a recent Web browser (Chrome 7 or later, Firefox 4 or later, or Internet Explorer 7 or later) with Adobe Flash Player version 10.2 or later installed
- A display that's 1024 × 768 or larger
- A reliable Internet connection
- A microphone and speakers (or headphones) to record and listen to music

Once you have a browser and Adobe Flash Player installed, just point your browser at *http://scratch.mit.edu/*. You can create a new Scratch project without logging in by clicking the **Create** button. You'll want to eventually **Join Scratch** to create your own account and save your projects (see how in "Join the Community!" on page 15).

You should download the projects used in this book from *http://nostarch.com/scratch/*. This online resource includes complete working projects, custom sprites, and a short *Getting Started with Scratch* guide produced by the Scratch team.

NOTE   *The Resources file includes two versions of each game in the book. One version is a completely finished and playable game, perfect for young learners and anyone who wants to build on the games in the book. The second set of projects has no programming added, so that students can follow along with the programming instructions in this book. Remember, there's no wrong way to play with Scratch!*

BUT WHAT IS SCRATCH, ANYWAY?

Scratch is a graphical programming language that you can use for free. By simply dragging and dropping colored blocks, you can create interactive stories, games, animation, music, art, and presentations. You can even upload your creations to the Internet to share them with Scratch programmers from around the world. Scratch is designed for play, self-directed learning, and design.

WHERE DID THE NAME SCRATCH COME FROM?

Scratch is named for the way that hip-hop disc jockeys (DJs) creatively combine pieces of music, using a technique called *scratching*. In the same way, Scratch programmers join different media (images, photos, sound effects, and so on) in exciting ways to create something entirely new.

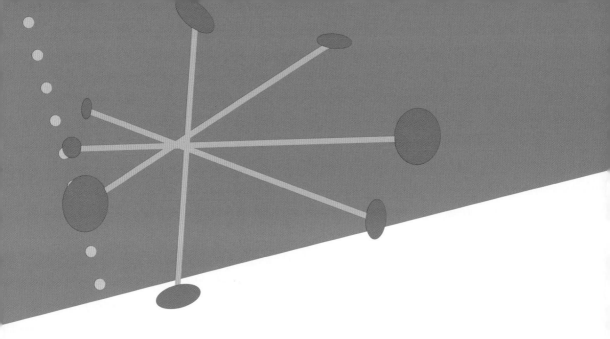

WHO CREATED SCRATCH?

Scratch is a project funded by the US National Science Foundation (NSF). It was developed by the Massachusetts Institute of Technology (MIT) Media Lab's Lifelong Kindergarten Group.

WHO IS SCRATCH FOR?

Scratch was developed for young people aged 8 and up to help them develop creative learning skills for the 21st century. When kids create programs, they learn important mathematical and computer concepts that improve their creative thinking, logical reasoning, problem solving, and collaboration skills.

This creative thinking spiral is from Professor Resnick's article, "Sowing the Seeds of a More Creative Society," published in *ISTE (International Society for Technology in Education)*.

Designing Scratch projects challenges kids to think creatively, and learning how to overcome obstacles and solve problems builds confidence. This gives learners an advantage later in life.

IS IT EASY TO USE SCRATCH?

Scratch was designed to prevent the common beginner pitfalls in traditional programming languages, like misspelling and errors in consistency. Instead of typing commands, programming in Scratch is performed by dragging and joining programming blocks. This graphical interface allows users to easily control the way in which different types of commands react to each other. Additionally, each block can fit with another only if it makes computational sense. Colorized categories help organize and group different sets of related commands based on their particular functions.

Since programs in Scratch run in real time, they can be edited and tested at any given moment, even while the program is running. This allows users to easily experiment with new ideas or to repeatedly test their improvements!

HOW MANY LANGUAGES DOES SCRATCH SUPPORT?

Scratch can be used in 50 different languages. Choose your language from the pull-down menu at the bottom of the Scratch website.

WHERE CAN YOU USE SCRATCH?

You can use Scratch at schools, libraries, community centers, and home. Even though Scratch is designed for young people aged 8 and up, younger children can also learn to design and create alongside their parents or siblings.

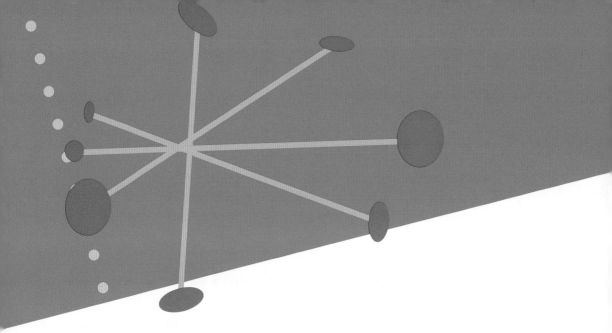

Scratch is used around the world in elementary, middle, and high schools. Computer science professors also use Scratch as a means of introducing programming concepts to college students.

HOW CAN SCRATCH BE USED TO EDUCATE IN SCHOOLS?

Schools can use Scratch to aid teachers in subjects like mathematics, English, music, art, design, and information technology. Scratch is designed for exploration and experimentation, so it supports many different learning styles.

No matter what they use Scratch for—creative storytelling, unique video games, or simple demonstrations of programming concepts—Scratch will provide a space for students to explore and imagine. By engaging in design-based activity individually or in groups, students will be motivated to learn.

Here are just a few of the things that students have used Scratch to do:

- A school in New York City used Scratch to build simulations of the spread of infectious diseases.
- A group of teenagers in India used Scratch to make an animated map of their village, illustrating environmental concerns where they live.

- Students at a university in Istanbul used Scratch to examine video game culture by rapidly prototyping their own games and testing the games with the public.
- English students in a middle school in California used Scratch to build a random story generator.
- Students in an elementary school in Russia used Scratch to build their own personalized tutorials for learning about the coordinate system and trigonometry.
- High school students in Michigan used Scratch to build a physics simulator.

The possibilities are endless. It is our sincere hope that this book inspires students to create their own games, stories, and more.

JOIN THE COMMUNITY!

Because Scratch is online, kids can easily share their own Scratch projects with their friends, family, and teachers. Once someone shares their work publicly on the Scratch website, other Scratch programmers can remix their projects, give them feedback, and more.

Follow these steps to join Scratch:

1. Visit the Scratch home page (*http://scratch.mit.edu/*) and click **Join Scratch** to register (you only need to register once).

2. Choose a username (don't use your real name), and then fill out the rest of the information. If the person registering is under 13, Scratch will ask for the email address of a parent or guardian.

NOTE *Once you share a project, everyone in the whole world can see what you've made! Make sure that your kids or students know to keep their personal information private.*

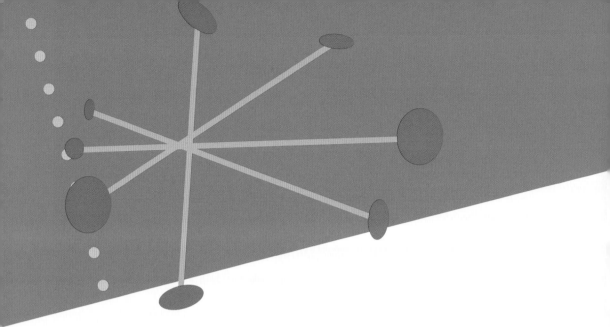

As long as they have the username and password at hand, kids can find games to play through the project gallery, remix them, and share their thoughts with others from around the world! To see how someone else's game was built, just click the **See Inside** button (See inside). To add to the program, click the big orange **Remix** button (Remix).

To share your own projects with the rest of the world, click the big **Share** button (Share) in the Scratch editor. To make a project private again, click the **Unshare** button in the **My Stuff** listing.

Just remember that as a member of the Scratch community, you'll be sharing projects and ideas with people of all ages, all levels of experience, and all parts of the world. So be sure to:

- Be respectful of other players
- Be constructive when commenting
- Help keep the site friendly and fun
- Keep personal information private

For more ideas and information about sharing and remixing projects, visit *http://wiki.scratch.mit.edu/wiki/Remix*.

MY COMPUTER CAN'T RUN SCRATCH 2.0!

If your computer doesn't meet the requirements listed on page 10, you can still download and install Scratch 1.4. (*http://scratch.mit.edu/scratch_1.4/*). Scratch 1.4 projects are compatible with the Web-based Scratch 2.0, and you can still share your projects on the Scratch website using Scratch 1.4. (Unfortunately, Scratch 1.4 cannot read programs created in the Scratch 2.0 software.)

You can download free PDF versions of Chapters 1 and 2, which explain how the older 1.4 interface works, by visiting *http://nostarch.com/scratch/*. You can also find versions of the book's games that are compatible with 1.4 on that page.

I'M AN EDUCATOR USING SCRATCH

Awesome! This book is great place to start for classes and after-school programs. You'll want to download the free Educator's Guide at *http://nostarch.com/scratch/*. Visit the official Scratch educator's forum at *http://scratched.media.mit.edu/* to exchange resources, share success stories, and ask questions of other educators already using Scratch as an educational tool.

I STILL HAVE OTHER QUESTIONS...

You can find more information on the Scratch website:

- Visit the Scratch FAQ at *http://info.scratch.mit.edu/Support/Scratch_FAQ/*.
- Visit the Scratch Help at *http://scratch.mit.edu/help/*.

"Online Resources" on page 156 has other helpful links. For updates to this book, visit *http://nostarch.com/scratch/*.

MEET THE CAST

Mitch
A computer science student who loves to make cool programs, he's passionate about movies and art, too! Mitch is an all-around good guy.

The Cosmic Defenders: Gobo, Fabu, and Pele
The Cosmic Defenders are transdimensional space aliens who can travel through space and time. Formally deputized by the Galactic Council, the Cosmic Defender's duty is to maintain the balance of the universe.

Scratchy
An energetic cat living in cyberspace, Scratchy is exactly what you'd expect from a cat on the Internet. He's quite curious and impulsive.

The Dark Wizard
He is a shapeless yet powerful and vengeful spirit, whose origins are unknown. Nothing can stop his ambition of destroying the order of space and time.

The Dark Minions
These pesky foes are Cosmic Defenders who have fallen to the dark side. They work for the Dark Wizard now.

RIDING A FLARE FROM THE SUN

A SOLAR STORM RAGES ON THE SURFACE OF THE SUN....

A FLARE EXPLODES WITH A BURST OF ENERGY!

BEOOO- BEOOOOP!

MEANWHILE, IN SCHOOL ON EARTH...

I SURE WISH PROGRAMMING WERE EASIER...

EARTHQUAKE!

WHOA!

CHIRP CHIRP

WAKE UP.

COME ON, WAKE UP!

W-WHO ARE YOU? WHAT JUST HAPPENED?

MY NAME IS SCRATCHY. I'M FROM CYBERSPACE.

YOU'RE FROM A COMPUTER?!

THAT'S RIGHT. I FOLLOWED THAT FLASH OF LIGHT, AND HERE I AM!

AMAZING! MY NAME IS MITCH. I'M A COMPUTER SCIENCE STUDENT!

HEY MITCH. UM...IS YOUR PLANET ALWAYS SO GRAY?

NO WAY! SOMETHING'S WRONG. LET'S GO CHECK IT OUT!

WHERE IS EVERYBODY?

SOMETHING TERRIBLE IS FORMING IN THE SKY!

OH NO! I CAN'T MOVE MY LEGS!

AHHH! ME NEITHER! HELP!!

STAY CALM! THANK GOODNESS I FOUND YOU!

YOUR BODY IS BEING FROZEN!

TAKE THIS SECRET MANUAL BEFORE THE BLACK TORNADO SWALLOWS YOU! THEN FOLLOW MY INSTRUCTIONS!

LET'S DO THIS!

BREAKING THE SPELL!

STAGE 1

➕ Chapter Focus

Let's get to know Scratch! We'll also learn about *sprites* and *coordinates*.

✏️ The Game

We need to get Scratchy the cat moving again. We'll make him dance across the Stage.

To follow along with the Secret Manual, you first need to open Scratch. Once you **Create** a new project, you'll see Scratchy the cat on a white backdrop. The cat doesn't do anything yet because he doesn't have any programs. Scratch calls Scratchy the cat—and all the other characters and objects we add to a project—a *sprite*. Soon, we'll start giving him directions to move by using the blue blocks in the middle of the screen.

The command blocks you can give a sprite are here. We'll stack these commands together to break the magic spell and get Scratchy back on his feet. The blocks here are all blue, as they're from the **Motion** palette.

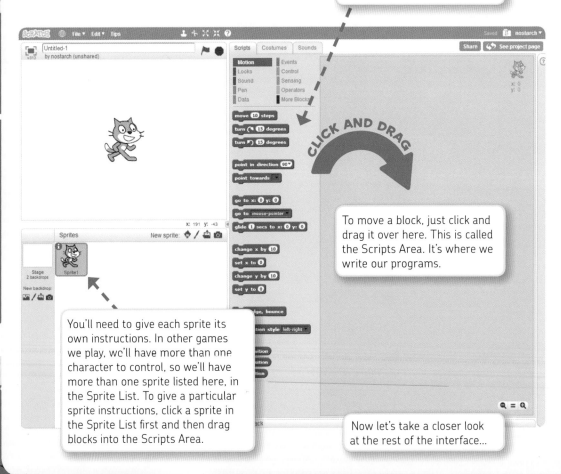

CLICK AND DRAG

To move a block, just click and drag it over here. This is called the Scripts Area. It's where we write our programs.

You'll need to give each sprite its own instructions. In other games we play, we'll have more than one character to control, so we'll have more than one sprite listed here, in the Sprite List. To give a particular sprite instructions, click a sprite in the Sprite List first and then drag blocks into the Scripts Area.

Now let's take a closer look at the rest of the interface...

A Guided Tour of the Scratch Interface!

Play the game full screen.

Give your project a new name.

Sprite Toolbar
Contains the Duplicate, Delete, Grow, Shrink, and Block Help tools

Palette
Each of these ten buttons lets you choose functions (called *blocks*) for programming your sprites. You can combine these command blocks in stacks to create programs that control objects on the screen.

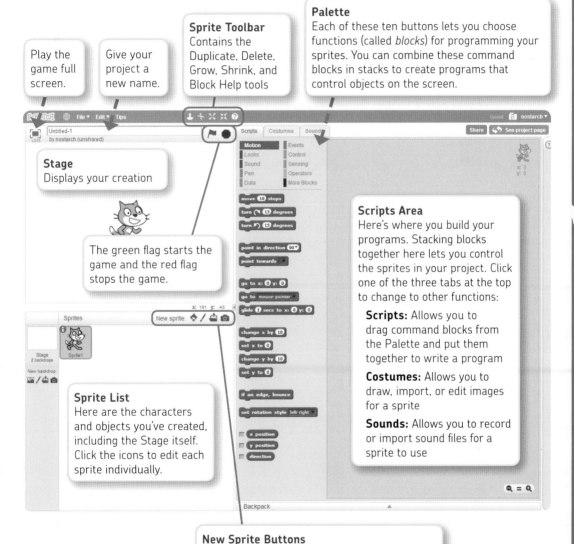

Stage
Displays your creation

The green flag starts the game and the red flag stops the game.

Sprite List
Here are the characters and objects you've created, including the Stage itself. Click the icons to edit each sprite individually.

Scripts Area
Here's where you build your programs. Stacking blocks together here lets you control the sprites in your project. Click one of the three tabs at the top to change to other functions:

Scripts: Allows you to drag command blocks from the Palette and put them together to write a program

Costumes: Allows you to draw, import, or edit images for a sprite

Sounds: Allows you to record or import sound files for a sprite to use

New Sprite Buttons
There are four ways to add a sprite:
• Pick one from Scratch's built-in library
• Draw a new one
• Upload an image you already have
• Take a photo with your computer's webcam

Sprite Information

You might have noticed a little blue **i** in the corner of the box around Scratchy when you select his sprite in the Sprite List. Try clicking the **i**, and you'll get information about that sprite.

This section shows the sprite's name, position, and direction it is facing (the little blue line).

This is how you can rename the Scratchy sprite. Right now it's *Sprite1*. Don't you think that's a little boring? Try renaming this sprite.

CLICK HERE

Sprites   New sprite:

Supreme Cat #1

x: 0   y: 0   direction: 90°

rotation style: ↻ ↔ •

can drag in player: ☐

show: ☑

Click this arrow when you're done with the Sprite Settings pane. We'll play with these other settings later.

Rotation Settings

You can control how a sprite rotates in three ways:
- Can rotate freely
- Can face only left or right
- No rotating allowed

Try clicking and dragging the little blue line—see what happens to Scratchy's orientation.

Now, onto the fun stuff. To use Scratch to program movements, you first have to understand how Scratch positions things.

Click the **Stage** icon in the Sprite List. Switch to the **Backdrops** tab in the Scripts Area and choose **Choose backdrop from library**.

Note: Sprites have *costumes* while the Stage has *backdrops*.

Scripts   Backdrops   Sounds

New backdrop: backdrop1

1

backdrop1
480x360

Stage
2 backdrops

New backdrop:

Choose the *xy-grid* backdrop and click **OK** to use it. It's in the "Other" category.

Backdrop Library

Category
  All
  Indoors
  Outdoors
  Other
Theme

xy-grid

Now you can see exactly how Scratch positions objects. Everything is on a grid with two axes:

y-axis: A vertical line that marks up and down positions; ranges from –180 (lowest) to +180 (highest)

x-axis: A horizontal line that marks left and right positions; ranges from –240 (farthest left) to +240 (farthest right)

Scratchy's default position is at the point where the x-axis and y-axis meet. His coordinates are (X: 0, Y: 0).

Now we can program movements for Scratchy the cat! But first, try dragging him to the top of the Stage, as shown on the right.

Note: The bottom-right corner displays the coordinates of your mouse. This will be really helpful when we start setting the positions of sprites!

The current coordinates of a sprite are shown in the upper-right corner of the Scripts Area, too.

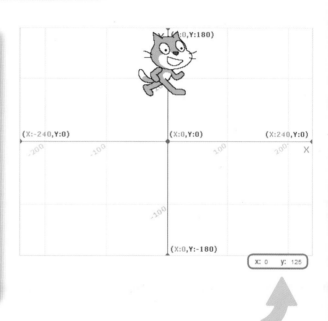

(X:0,Y:180)
(X:-240,Y:0)   (X:0,Y:0)   (X:240,Y:0)
-200   -100   100   200   X
-100
(X:0,Y:-180)

x: 0   y: 125

x: 0
y: 125

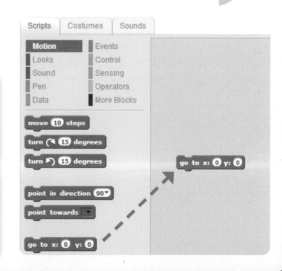

Scripts   Costumes   Sounds

Motion	Events
Looks	Control
Sound	Sensing
Pen	Operators
Data	More Blocks

move 10 steps

turn ↻ 15 degrees

turn ↺ 15 degrees

go to x: 0 y: 0

point in direction 90▾

point towards ▾

go to x: 0 y: 0

To make sure we're giving Scratchy the cat instructions, click him in the Sprite List (the box at the bottom left of the screen). Switch to the **Scripts** tab in the Scripts Area and then click the **Motion** palette button. Click and drag out the command block go to x:0 y:0 to the Scripts Area.

Sprite1

Click the number of a coordinate to change it. Set x to 0 and set y to 125. Now click the block to run it! Scratch goes right to that position. We've just written our first program! It's really that simple.

We want Scratchy to move around, but at the moment, he moves too fast for us to see! To make him move more slowly, click the **Control** palette and drag out the command wait 1 secs to the Scripts Area. Make sure to drag it under your blue command block. Wait for a white line to appear and then release the mouse.

The two commands are joined together! Now change the time to 0.1 secs.

Tip: If you want to separate the commands, simply drag away the block. If you want to delete a block, simply drag it back to the palette. Give it a try. To move a big stack of blocks, click and drag the topmost block in the stack.

Next, select the **Duplicate** button on the Sprite Toolbar and stamp it on the commands to make five copies.

Type these coordinates in your own program, so it matches this picture. When you're finished, click the whole command block to make Scratchy jump around in a pentagon shape!

```
go to x: 150 y: 30
wait 0.1 secs
go to x: 100 y: -120
wait 0.1 secs
go to x: -100 y: -120
wait 0.1 secs
go to x: -150 y: 30
wait 0.1 secs
```

To make him move in a loop continuously, drag out the command block forever from the **Control** palette and place it at the top of the code. Click the block, and it will actually run! Click to stop Scratchy from moving around. You can test any program in this way—just click it with your mouse.

Tip: Whenever you're writing scripts, you'll want to test them every now and then to see if they work the way you expect.

```
forever
    go to x: 0 y: 125
    wait 0.1 secs
    go to x: 150 y: 30
    wait 0.1 secs
    go to x: 100 y: -120
    wait 0.1 secs
    go to x: -100 y: -120
    wait 0.1 secs
    go to x: -150 y: 30
    wait 0.1 secs
```

Now let's make Scratchy glide around instead of jumping from point to point. To do this, click the **Motion** palette, drag out five glide commands, and join them together. Follow the picture on the right, and copy the seconds and coordinates. Once you're finished, click the script to see the results!

```
glide 0.1 secs to x: 150 y: 30
glide 0.1 secs to x: -100 y: -120
glide 0.1 secs to x: 0 y: 125
glide 0.1 secs to x: 100 y: -120
glide 0.1 secs to x: -150 y: 30
```

Now we can join these two programs together! From the **Events** palette, drag out the When 🏳 clicked command and put it at the top of your two scripts.

Tip: We'll often need multiple scripts to start at the same time, and using the When 🏳 clicked command will help us do that.

```
when      clicked
forever
    go to x: 0 y: 125
    wait 0.1 secs
    go to x: 150 y: 30
    wait 0.1 secs
    go to x: 100 y: -120
    wait 0.1 secs
    go to x: -100 y: -120
    wait 0.1 secs
    go to x: -150 y: 30
    wait 0.1 secs
    glide 0.1 secs to x: 150 y: 30
    glide 0.1 secs to x: -100 y: -120
    glide 0.1 secs to x: 0 y: 125
    glide 0.1 secs to x: 100 y: -120
    glide 0.1 secs to x: -150 y: 30
```

Because we used the `When` 🚩 `clicked` command, we can use these buttons above the Stage to start (🚩) and stop (⬤) the game.

Next, click the **Pen** palette and drag out the four green Pen blocks shown on the right. Now when Scratchy moves, he'll draw a *magic star web*!

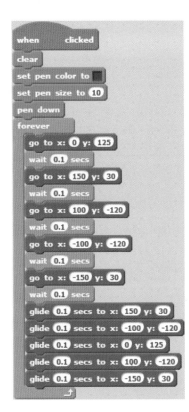

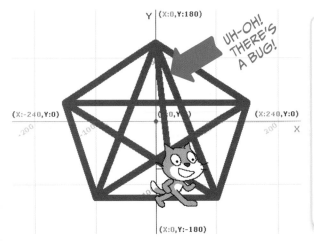

UH-OH! THERE'S A BUG!

Occasionally, when you run your program, there is a *software bug*. This is the most exciting part of computer programming: discovering an error in something you have made and then solving the problem. In this case, sometimes Scratchy will draw an odd line at the beginning of the program.

If we drag Scratchy anywhere else on the Stage and then press 🚩, he draws an extra line because he starts in the wrong place. Try doing this multiple times to see if you can spot the bug.

This software bug can be fixed by adding some more code—that is, new blocks—to your program. In this case, simply place a new `go to` block (from the blue **Motion** palette) above the green Pen blocks and below the `When ⚑ clicked` block.

With this little correction, Scratchy will always begin drawing from the correct position in the grid. The bug is gone!

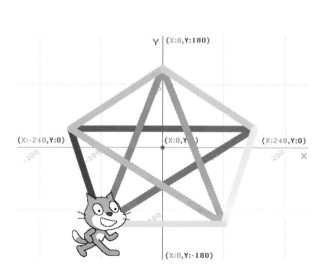

Let's add a whole new program to make a magic star web that changes colors. Build a second stack of blocks that uses the `change pen color by` command and see what happens.

Isn't that cool? You can give a single sprite more than one set of blocks! Scratchy now has two programs. This tiny second program sure makes a big difference in how the game looks.

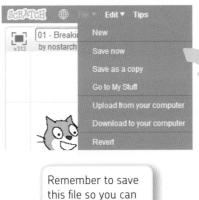

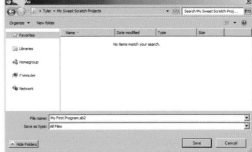

Remember to save this file so you can play with it later!

If you are logged into Scratch, the website stores all of your projects into **My Stuff** so you can easily find them. The website saves your progress every so often, but you can save manually too: **File ▸ Save Now**. You can also save different versions of your programs to make sure you don't lose older versions of your games and can safely experiment—**File ▸ Save Copy** creates a new version of your project in My Stuff. If you want to download a version for yourself, try **File ▸ Download to your computer**. Then save it in a safe spot!

Scratchy's Challenge!!

Can you edit this program to make Scratchy draw different kinds of shapes? Give it a try!

ENTERING SPACE

2 STAGE

STAGE 2

MAGIC STAR WEB!

WHOOSH

ALRIGHT! I CAN FEEL MY LIMBS AGAIN!

NICE WORK! YOU'VE BROKEN THE DARK WIZARD'S SPELL!

THE DARK WIZARD?

WHO ARE YOU AGAIN?

MY NAME IS GOBO. I'M A COSMIC DEFENDER!

THAT SOLAR FLARE DESTROYED THE BALANCE BETWEEN THE DIGITAL WORLD AND THE REAL WORLD!

THIS UNIVERSE IS NOW CONTROLLED BY THE DARK WIZARD AND HIS MINIONS. THEY FROZE ALL THE COSMIC DEFENDERS BESIDES ME— AND ALL THE HUMANS ON EARTH.

OH NO! WE'RE THE ONLY ONES LEFT!

THIS SECRET MANUAL SAVED US. MAYBE IT CAN HELP OTHER PEOPLE AS WELL!

YES! IF I LEARN TO PROGRAM, IT MIGHT HELP TO DEFEAT THE DARK WIZARD!

GREAT IDEA! YOU CAN DESIGN NEW EQUIPMENT AND EVEN CONTROL OUR MOVEMENTS!

OH NO! MY FELLOW DEFENDERS ARE IN TROUBLE! CHANGE INTO A SPACE SUIT AND SAVE THEM, KIND FELINE!

ALRIGHT! BUT WHY DOES SCRATCHY NEED THE SPACE SUIT?

WE NEED THE ENERGY FROM SEVEN DIMENSIONAL STRINGS TO OPEN THE STARGATE AND REACH MY FRIENDS...

...BUT INSIDE THE VORTEX, THERE'S NO OXYGEN, AND LIGHTNING CAN MAKE THINGS DISAPPEAR!

I'M READY!

BY THE WAY, GOBO, MY NAME IS SCRATCHY, AND HE'S MITCH!

WOW! IT'S FULL OF STARS!

THE ADVENTURE INTO SPACE BEGINS...

A SPACE ODYSSEY!

2 STAGE

Chapter Focus

Learn to design new costumes and program a sprite's movements, reactions, and sound effects.

The Game

Avoid the lightning bolts and collect seven dimensional strings. Once you've got them all, the Monolith will appear!

To make things really easy, let's start by opening a blank project called **02 - A Space Odyssey.sb2**. This project has all the sprites you'll need, but none of the programming yet. To open a file, click **File ▸ Upload from your computer**.

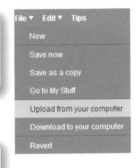

But let's try making some sprites of our own, so you can make changes to this game's characters and invent your own games, too! Click Scratchy's sprite icon in the Sprite List, and then click the **Costumes** tab. You'll see the Paint Editor—just be sure to click the costume you want to change.

At the top of the Paint Editor, you can give your Costume a name. We can then reference the costume names in our programming.

If your Paint Editor looks different, it could be because you haven't opened the blank project file (*02 - A Space Odyssey .sb2*) that has Scratchy's astronaut costume.

Scratch has two modes for editing graphics— on the right is **Bitmap** mode. See page 38 to learn more about editing in Vector mode.

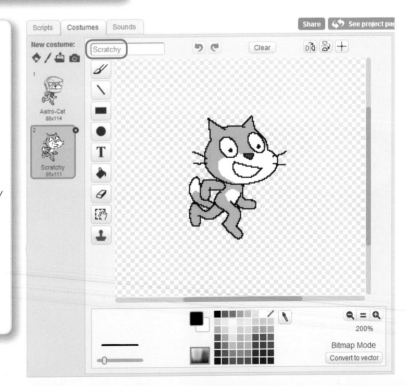

Here's where all the tools are. The **Brush** and **Eraser** tools make it easy to draw.

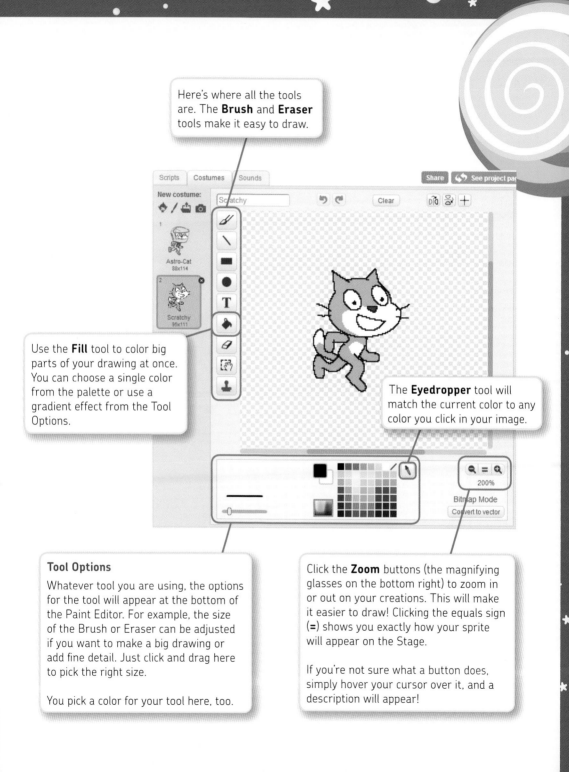

Use the **Fill** tool to color big parts of your drawing at once. You can choose a single color from the palette or use a gradient effect from the Tool Options.

The **Eyedropper** tool will match the current color to any color you click in your image.

Tool Options

Whatever tool you are using, the options for the tool will appear at the bottom of the Paint Editor. For example, the size of the Brush or Eraser can be adjusted if you want to make a big drawing or add fine detail. Just click and drag here to pick the right size.

You pick a color for your tool here, too.

Click the **Zoom** buttons (the magnifying glasses on the bottom right) to zoom in or out on your creations. This will make it easier to draw! Clicking the equals sign (**=**) shows you exactly how your sprite will appear on the Stage.

If you're not sure what a button does, simply hover your cursor over it, and a description will appear!

You also have tools to draw rectangles and ellipses. Can you give Scratchy a stovepipe hat like Abe Lincoln using the **Rectangle** and **Ellipse** tools?

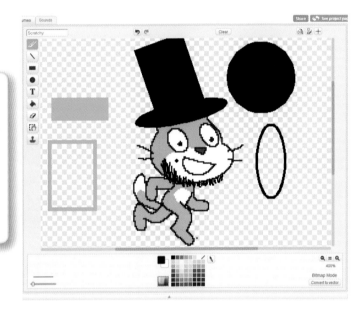

These shapes can be empty inside or filled in. Try experimenting with different colors for the inside and outside. If you press the SHIFT key when you start to draw, you'll have a perfect circle or square! (You can also use this SHIFT trick when using the **Line** tool to draw a straight line.) Try rotating your shapes using the handle on the top of the box.

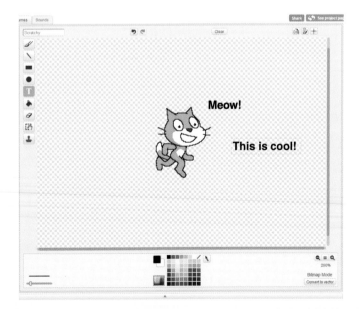

The **Text** tool lets you add writing to your sprite. We'll use this tool when we need to give the player instructions for our games. If you want to move the text, simply click and drag the black box that surrounds your text.

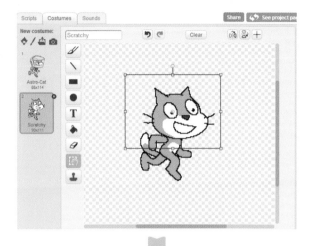

To use the **Select** tool, use your mouse to create a frame around a certain area. Then you can do all sorts of things to the selected part of your costume:

- Click and drag the selection to move it to a new location.
- Resize, smush, or stretch the image using the handles on the sides of the box
- Rotate the selection by clicking and dragging the handle at the top center of the box
- Press and hold the CTRL key and C key at the same time to copy the image area (Mac users can use ⌘-C instead). Then press CTRL-V to paste your selection, as many times as you like.
- Press the DELETE key to erase the selection.

The **Set costume center** button marks the center of your sprite. This helps to make sure your sprite doesn't end up in the wrong place when it spins or rotates!

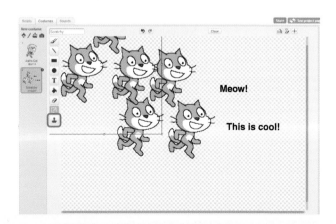

By using the **Duplicate** tool, you can copy and stamp a selected area as many times as you want! Just draw a frame around the area you want to copy and then click wherever you want to paste.

Vector Mode

You may have noticed that when you edit other sprites in Scratch, you don't see the same Paint Editor tools. Some newer sprites are *vector* art—that's just a fancy way to say they're made of shapes, instead of pixels. Vector art have small filesizes, but they are great quality—and they can be resized without losing quality.

Note: For simplicity's sake, all of the graphics in this book use Bitmap mode. But your custom projects can use a mix of vector and bitmap graphics.

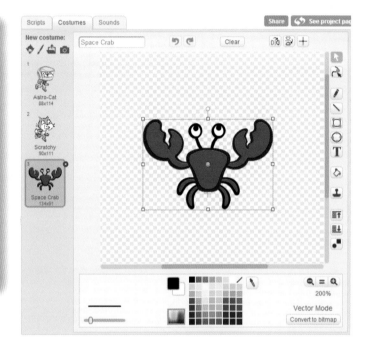

You can switch from Scratch's **Bitmap** mode (the one seen earlier) to **Vector** mode by clicking the **Convert to Vector** button at the bottom right of the Paint Editor. The difference between using these two tools in Scratch is like the difference between Adobe Photoshop and Illustrator—or GIMP and Inkscape. Use whichever Paint Editor mode you like the most!

You can import SVG files into Scratch's vector editor. In Vector mode, you can squeeze and shape lines, reshape, and ungroup. Here's how the Vector mode works.

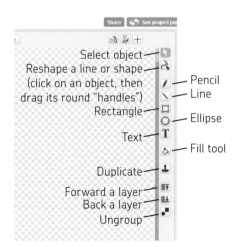

Try opening a vector graphic from Scratch's library, and give editing one a try.

 butterfly3

 cat1-a

 cat1-b

 cat2

 crab-a

 dinosaur1-a

 dinosaur1-b

 dinosaur1-c

dinosaur1-d

 dinosaur1-e

The Backpack

Here's a cool new feature. If you're logged into the Scratch website, you'll see something called the **Backpack** at the very bottom of the screen. Click it, and it'll open up. Yours will be empty until you throw some sprites in it.

Your Backpack lets you share sprites and scripts between projects. If you play a really cool game on the Scratch website and want to use the character in an entirely new project, just click and drag the sprite right into your Backpack.

When you create a new project of your own, just open the Backpack again and drag the sprite out. You can write all new programs, or use the ones that were already with the sprite. You can even use your Backpack to store programs you want to reuse!

Once you know how to use the Paint Editor's tools, Scratchy can put on his space suit! Go ahead and draw your own, or use the costume that's already in the project.

Because we've selected the horizontal rotation style (circled below) Scratchy will face only left and right.

Now we have the main character for our game: Scratchy the astronaut!

Next, let's take a look at the other sprites in the game. You can use the art that's already in the game, or draw new artwork yourself! Click 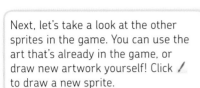 to draw a new sprite.

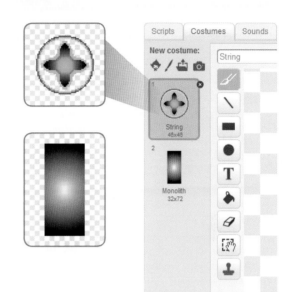

First, take a look at the String and the Monolith. They are two costumes for the same sprite, **String**. If they were two separate sprites, we'd have to write two programs. But now we can make this sprite switch costumes and write only one program.

Now for our third new sprite, some scary **Lightning**! The player will need to avoid the lighting.

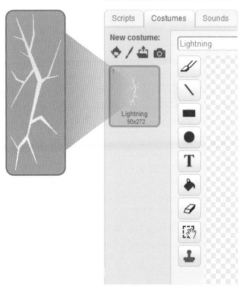

We also need some instructions to appear at the start of the game. We'll call this sprite **Banner**.

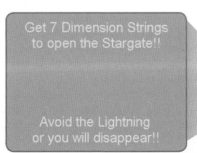

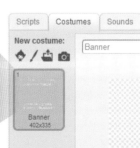

Next, let's look at the Stage.
I used artwork of a black hole
from NASA! You can draw a
new backdrop if you like. Click
the Stage in the Sprite List, and
then click the **Backdrops** tab.

Stage
1 backdrop

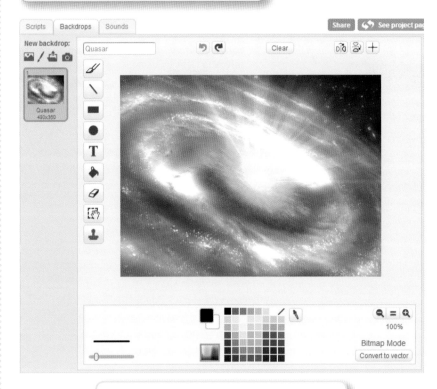

Now that we have a bunch of sprites for the
game, you can see how everything appears in
the Sprite List. To give a sprite new instructions
or costumes, you'll first have to click it in the
Sprite List. Let's start by giving Scratchy the
astronaut his programming.

Let's write our first program ❶ for Scratchy! Make
sure he's selected in the Sprite List and you've clicked
the **Scripts** tab. His first program is a short one that
makes him bounce up and down a little. This makes
him look like he's floating in zero gravity!

Astro-Cat

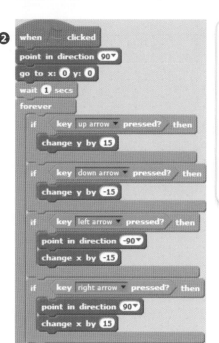

2
```
when  clicked
point in direction (90▼)
go to x: (0) y: (0)
wait (1) secs
forever
    if    key (up arrow ▼) pressed?  then
        change y by (15)

    if    key (down arrow ▼) pressed?  then
        change y by (-15)

    if    key (left arrow ▼) pressed?  then
        point in direction (-90▼)
        change x by (-15)

    if    key (right arrow ▼) pressed?  then
        point in direction (90▼)
        change x by (15)
```

For program **2**, we'll make a *conditional*—if something is true, then something else will happen. In the **Control** palette, drag out an `if` block. Then for the diamond shape, drag the **Sensing** block `key____pressed?`. Right below the `if`, put what you want to happen when the statement is true. Drag out the rest of these commands to form the complete program. Now you can move Scratchy up, down, left, and right by using the keyboard!

Now we'll give Scratchy two more programs. We'll need to program them individually, and then use `When ⚑ clicked` to make them all run at the same time.

3
```
when  clicked
switch costume to (Astro-Cat ▼)
forever
    go to front
```

Let's write programs **3** and **4**. Click the **Control** and **Looks** palettes and drag out these commands.

Program **3** controls which costume Scratchy wears, and program **4** makes Scratchy become invisible like a ghost each time he gets struck by lightning.

When you've finished all of this, Scratchy's programming is complete!

4
```
when  clicked
clear graphic effects
forever
    if    touching (Lightning ▼) ?  then
        repeat (10)
            change (ghost ▼) effect by (1)
```

Next, let's click the **Banner** sprite. We just need a simple program to make these instructions appear at the start of the game. The `repeat 2` loop using the `show` and `hide` blocks makes our instructions flash, so the game is even more exciting.

```
when  clicked
hide
go to x: (0) y: (0)
go to front
repeat (2)
    show
    wait (0.4) secs
    hide
    wait (0.1) secs
```

Now we can add sound effects to the game! I've already added a few, but you can change things up. First, click the **Stage** in the Sprite List. Then click its **Sounds** tab. You can create whatever kind of sounds effects or music you like for your Scratch projects. You can even record your own sounds right in the Scratch program.

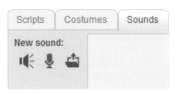

If you click the **Record** button, a sound recorder will pop up. You can click the round button to record speech or sound effects through a microphone. When you're finished, click **OK**.

Note: To record your own sounds, you'll need a microphone attached to the computer. To listen to sound effects and music, you'll need speakers.

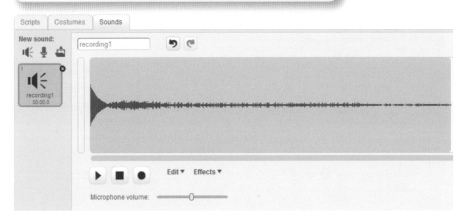

If you want to use sounds that are prerecorded, you can press ◀: to use Scratch's sound library, or ⬆ to choose files from your own computer (MP3 and compressed WAV, AIF, and AU formats are supported).

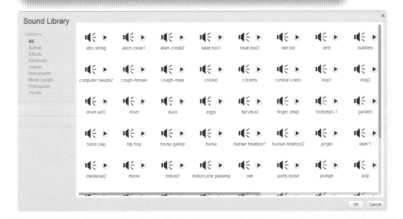

Now we can add some simple programs to the Stage. Program ① makes its backdrop change colors. In program ②, use the **Sound** palette to add a song to the Stage.

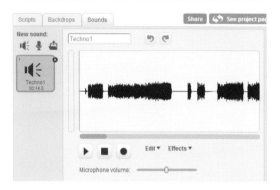

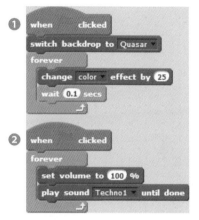

Next, we can add some sound effects to the String and Lightning sprites to make the game more exciting! Test how you like my sound effects, and make your own if you like.

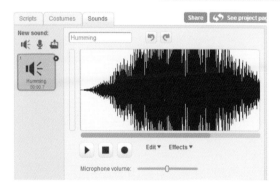

You can record a sound yourself and then change it using the **Effects** menu. Try reversing what you record to make it sound really weird!

Click the **Lightning** sprite, and write a program so that whenever Scratchy touches a lightning bolt, a sound will play.

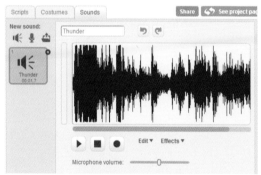

The **Lightning** sprite needs some more programs. Go to the **Control**, **Events**, **Looks**, and **Operators** palettes and program these commands to have the lightning bolt randomly grow bigger or smaller, making the game more magical.

```
when [ ] clicked
forever
    set size to (pick random 30 to 60) %
```

Next, write this program to make the lightning disappear whenever Scratchy touches it and to control the way it moves.

The lightning's vertical position (y-axis) changes because we repeat eight times the subtraction of 40 steps (-40) from its original y-coordinate of 260. To make the lightning move differently, you can change and play with these numbers.

So that the lightning bolt makes Scratchy disappear, we must make sure that each time it moves—that is, the position of its y-axis changes—the program will check if it touches Scratchy.

```
when [ ] clicked
hide
wait 1 secs
forever
    wait (pick random 0 to 1.5) secs
    go to x: (pick random -210 to 210) y: 260
    go to front
    go back 1 layers
    show
    repeat 8
        change y by -40
        wait 0.3 secs
        if < touching Astro-Cat ? > then
            hide
    hide
```

Tip: Sometimes when you've used the hide and show blocks, a sprite can disappear while you're working on the program—running it, testing it, and checking for bugs. Simply click the show block in the **Looks** palette to make the sprite appear again. (You can also check the **show** box in the Sprite Information pane.)

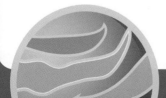

Now it's time to program the **String** sprite. Make sure you click it in the Sprite List first! Program ❶ makes it change color, just like our Stage. Program ❷ will give it a simple animation, using the fisheye effect.

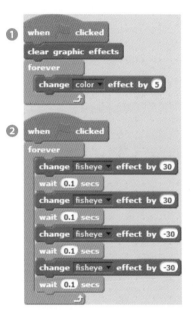

❶
```
when       clicked
clear graphic effects
forever
    change  color ▼  effect by  5
```

❷
```
when       clicked
forever
    change  fisheye ▼  effect by  30
    wait  0.1  secs
    change  fisheye ▼  effect by  30
    wait  0.1  secs
    change  fisheye ▼  effect by  -30
    wait  0.1  secs
    change  fisheye ▼  effect by  -30
    wait  0.1  secs
```

Now for a big program. Let's start by dragging out the blocks you can see in ❸. These will control how the String costume spins and moves.

❸
```
repeat until    touching  Astro-Cat ▼  ?
    change y by  1
    turn ↻  5  degrees
    wait  0.1  secs
    change y by  -1
    turn ↻  5  degrees
    wait  0.1  secs
```

Then add to your program so that it looks like ❹. This will make your dimensional string appear in a random place on the Stage seven different times. The say blocks and play sound blocks at the end of the program make sure the player knows he has grabbed a dimensional string.

❹
```
repeat 7
    go to x: pick random 210 to -210 y: pick random 150 to -150
    show
    repeat until   touching Astro-Cat ?
        change y by 1
        turn ↻ 5 degrees
        wait 0.1 secs
        change y by -1
        turn ↻ 5 degrees
        wait 0.1 secs
    say Got it!
    set volume to 30 %
    play sound Humming
    wait 0.2 secs
    say
    hide
    wait 0.3 secs
```

We're not done yet! This is a big script.

Add a `When ⚑ clicked` block at the top of our script and some instructions at the very bottom so that once Scratchy has collected seven dimensional strings, the String sprite will change to its Monolith costume. When that happens, the player wins the game. Make sure your finished program looks like ➎.

➎

```
when clicked
switch costume to String ▼
hide
wait 1 secs
repeat 7
    go to x: pick random 210 to -210 y: pick random 150 to -150
    show
    repeat until touching Astro-Cat ▼ ?
        change y by 1
        turn ↻ 5 degrees
        wait 0.1 secs
        change y by -1
        turn ↻ 5 degrees
        wait 0.1 secs
    say Got it!
    set volume to 30 %
    play sound Humming ▼
    wait 0.2 secs
    say
    hide
    wait 0.3 secs
go to x: 0 y: 0
point in direction 90 ▼
switch costume to Monolith ▼
go to front
go back 2 layers
show
say Stargate opened! for 2 secs
stop all ▼
```

Now you're done!
Nice work!

49

After saving the file, you can enjoy your final creation! Make the Stage full screen and click ⚑ to begin a new round.

Scratchy's Challenge!!

Add more lightning bolts to give yourself a challenge. Or you could replace the lightning bolt with a big, scary space monster you drew yourself! Give it a try!

TRAPPED BY MONA LISA'S SMILE

WOW, PARIS IS BEAUTIFUL!

THERE'S NO TIME TO SIGHTSEE! A COSMIC DEFENDER HAS BEEN TRAPPED IN MONA LISA'S SMILE!

HOW DEVIOUS!

THE STARGATE BROUGHT US TO PARIS...LET'S GO TO THE LOUVRE MUSEUM!

THE PAINTING'S IN THERE!

PUFF PUFF I SHOULD'VE TAKEN OFF THIS SPACE SUIT BEFORE RUNNING.

HOLD ON NOW. WE DARK MINIONS WON'T LET YOU IN SO EASILY!

RATA! BETRAYER! I CAN'T BELIEVE YOU'RE HELPING THE DARK WIZARD NOW!

ALL THE ART IN THE WORLD IS MINE NOW! *HEE HEE*

ART IS MEANT FOR SHARING. YOU CAN'T TAKE IT ALL FOR YOURSELF!

HUMPH! NOW THE PAINTING HOLDING YOUR FRIEND HAS BEEN CUT TO BITS! TAKE ON MY CHALLENGE AND THEN WE'LL TALK!

THE LOUVRE

STAGE 3

✚ Chapter Focus

Let's learn how to control the *flow* of a game. You'll see how to keep score using *variables* and control the order of the game using *broadcasts*.

✏ The Game

This game is actually two games in one. First, you'll face Rata's quiz. Then you'll have to put the *Mona Lisa* back together in a puzzle game. If you get the answer wrong three times, the game ends and you lose!

This program has some tricky custom graphics. So let's start out by opening a blank file called ***03 – Louvre Puzzle.sb2*** (File ▸ Upload from your computer), which has these sprites in it. Take a look around. You can see that the Stage has a backdrop that shows the Louvre. We just don't have any programs yet!

Then we'll add a program that makes the Stage play music. The `forever` block is a special kind of command we call a *loop*. Any sound effect or music you add here keeps playing again and again, so make sure you like how it sounds!

Photo Credit: Raphael Frey

Now click the sprite for **Rata**, in the Sprite List. Make sure you like how he looks. Since we selected him, now we can give him some programs!

| Scripts | Costumes | Sounds |

New costume:

Rata

1

Rata
126x123

Write program ❶ first. This forever loop makes Rata float up and down.

❶
```
when    clicked
forever
    change y by 2
    wait 0.3 secs
    change y by -2
    wait 0.3 secs
```

For program ❷, go to the **Looks**, **Sensing**, and **Operators** palettes, and use the `ask` and `say` blocks. This program asks the first question of Rata's quiz. We've made it a multiple-choice question, so the answer must be *A* or *B*.

❷
```
when    clicked
show
ask Who are you? and wait
say See if you can answer my questions, for 2 secs
say answer for 2 secs
forever
    ask Who painted "Mona Lisa"? (A) Leonardo da Vinci (B) Ludwig von Beethoven and wait
    if  answer = A  then
        say You are right! for 1 secs
        broadcast question2
        stop this script
    if  answer = B  then
        say Try again! for 1 secs
```

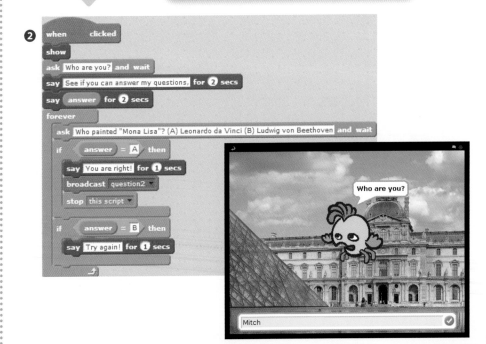

Who are you?

Mitch

If you noticed back in program **②**, there's a command that says `broadcast question2` if you get the right answer. *Broadcasts* are like big announcements to all the programs in your project. They're a great way to connect related parts of a game. So let's try writing two more questions as new programs **③** and **④**. These two programs wait for broadcasts `question2` and `question3` to start using the `when I receive` block.

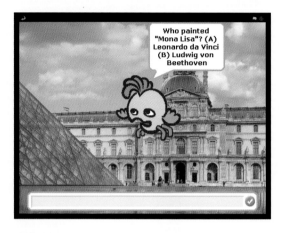

③
```
when I receive question2 ▼
forever
    ask Where was it painted? (A) Madrid, Spain (B) Florence, Italy and wait
    if    answer = A    then
        say Try again! for 1 secs

    if    answer = B    then
        say You are right! for 1 secs
        broadcast question3 ▼
        stop this script ▼
```

④
```
when I receive question3 ▼
forever
    ask Where is it now? (A) The Louvre, Paris (B) The Colosseum, Rome and wait
    if    answer = A    then
        say You are right! for 1 secs
        say Now try to solve this puzzle! for 2 secs
        hide
        broadcast puzzle ▼
        stop this script ▼

    if    answer = B    then
        say Try again! for 1 secs
```

When the player answers all three questions correctly, the `puzzle` broadcast signal in program **④** tells the game that the quiz is over and the puzzle half of our game should now begin.

1

Memorize the
picture sequence

instructions1
298x89

2

Repeat the sequence
correctly!

instructions2
356x89

3

monalisa1
119x180

4

monalisa2
119x180

5

monalisa3
119x180

6

monalisa4
119x180

7

↑ ■
↓ ■
← ■
→ ■

arrow_key
276x358

8

Start Now!

start
376x88

9

monalisa_win
238x360

10

monalisa_lose
245x360

Now take a look at the **Puzzle** sprite. This isn't just a single image—it's a sprite with a bunch of costumes. The sprite's costumes include instructions for the player, as well as the puzzle itself!

The final two costumes display the winning screen and the message that appears when you lose.

Let's take a closer look. First, we'll display the costume that shows instructions for the player.

Memorize the picture sequence!

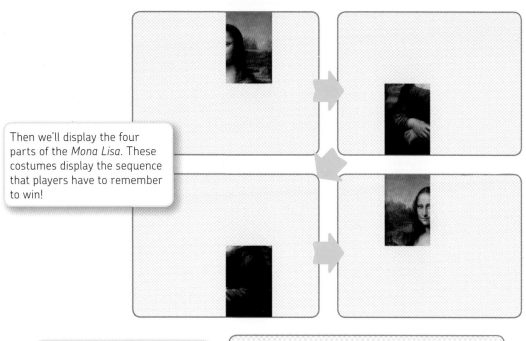

Then we'll display the four parts of the *Mona Lisa*. These costumes display the sequence that players have to remember to win!

The next three costumes display more game instructions and a start screen.

Repeat the sequence correctly!

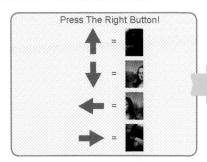

Start Now!!

YOU WIN!!

Finally, we have two costumes for the winning and losing screens.

YOU LOSE!!

For this big sprite, we'll need a lot of programs. Let's start by adding a special kind of command called a *variable*. Variables are good for keeping track of numbers that change during a game, like scores, player health, player lives, and more.

Click **Make a Variable** in the **Data** palette, and call it Chance. The new Chance variable is how the computer knows how many times the player gets another chance to solve the puzzle before losing.

Now for the programs themselves. Add scripts ❶ and ❷. Script ❶ just hides our variable Chance during the quiz part of the game. Next, script ❷ determines how the Puzzle sprite should change costumes—just as described on pages 56–57. After it's done switching costumes, it broadcasts start.

Then we'll add four different scripts: one for each right answer to the puzzle. If the player presses the wrong arrow, the sprite changes its costume and a broadcast called wrong is broadcast. We'll use this broadcast to control the Chance variable.

Tip: You can use the Duplicate tool (📥) in the Sprite Toolbar to save some time dragging out blocks.

Notice how the broadcast named 1 at the end of script ❸ starts script ❹. Likewise, script ❺ starts only when I receive 3, which is broadcast by script ❹ when the player presses the correct arrow. With all of the correct arrows pressed in script ❻, we signal a new broadcast called win.

❸
```
when I receive start
forever
  if key up arrow pressed? then
    switch costume to monalisa3
    say Sorry! for 1 secs
    broadcast wrong
  if key down arrow pressed? then
    switch costume to monalisa4
    say Sorry! for 1 secs
    broadcast wrong
  if key left arrow pressed? then
    switch costume to monalisa1
    say Correct! for 1 secs
    broadcast 1
    stop this script
  if key right arrow pressed? then
    switch costume to monalisa2
    say Sorry! for 1 secs
    broadcast wrong
```

❹
```
when I receive 1
forever
  if key up arrow pressed? then
    switch costume to monalisa3
    say Sorry! for 1 secs
    broadcast wrong
  if key down arrow pressed? then
    switch costume to monalisa4
    say Sorry! for 1 secs
    broadcast wrong
  if key left arrow pressed? then
    switch costume to monalisa1
    say Sorry! for 1 secs
    broadcast wrong
  if key right arrow pressed? then
    switch costume to monalisa2
    say Correct! for 1 secs
    broadcast 2
    stop this script
```

❺
```
when I receive 2
forever
  if key up arrow pressed? then
    switch costume to monalisa3
    say Correct! for 1 secs
    broadcast 3
    stop this script
  if key down arrow pressed? then
    switch costume to monalisa4
    say Sorry! for 1 secs
    broadcast wrong
  if key left arrow pressed? then
    switch costume to monalisa1
    say Sorry! for 1 secs
    broadcast wrong
  if key right arrow pressed? then
    switch costume to monalisa2
    say Sorry! for 1 secs
    broadcast wrong
```

❻
```
when I receive 3
forever
  if key up arrow pressed? then
    switch costume to monalisa3
    say Sorry! for 1 secs
    broadcast wrong
  if key down arrow pressed? then
    switch costume to monalisa4
    say Correct! for 1 secs
    broadcast win
    stop this script
  if key left arrow pressed? then
    switch costume to monalisa1
    say Sorry! for 1 secs
    broadcast wrong
  if key right arrow pressed? then
    switch costume to monalisa2
    say Sorry! for 1 secs
    broadcast wrong
```

⑦
```
when I receive wrong ▼
change Chance ▼ by -1
wait 1 secs
```

⑧
```
when 🚩 clicked
set Chance ▼ to 3
forever
  if   Chance < 1  then
    switch costume to monalisa_lose ▼
    stop all ▼
```

⑨
```
when I receive win ▼
switch costume to monalisa_win ▼
stop all ▼
```

Finally, add three more programs to the Puzzle. Program ⑦ subtracts 1 from the Chance variable any time it receives the wrong broadcast. Programs ⑧ and ⑨ control when the winning and losing screens appear.

That's it! Remember to save your project, and then give the game a try. Let's see if you can win this!

Scratchy's Challenge!!

Can you use the ask block and broadcasts to create a personality test? How about a flash-card game to learn words in a new language? Give it a try!

DEFEND HONG KONG'S TECHNOCORE

MISSION COMPLETED!

FABU'S FREE AGAIN!

SNIFF FOILED AGAIN...

AWW...DON'T BE UPSET! I JUST THINK THAT ART'S MEANT TO BE SHARED!

DO YOU THINK THE COSMIC DEFENDERS WOULD TAKE ME BACK... OR JUST FORGIVE ME... IF I APOLOGIZED?

PROBABLY! BUT BE CAREFUL NOW. NEWS HAS IT THAT THE DARK WIZARD IS PLANNING TO LAUNCH A VIRUS ATTACK ON HONG KONG!

OH NO! BUT IF THAT HAPPENS, THE WHOLE DIGITAL WORLD COULD BE DESTROYED!

FABU'S RIGHT! WE HAVE TO DESTROY THE VIRUS RIGHT AWAY!

HONG KONG

HERE IT COMES!

STAND BACK. I KNOW KUNG FU!

HACK ATTACK

Chapter Focus

Learn to control sprites with the mouse, program objects to bounce back, and start a game by pressing the spacebar.

The Game

Help Scratchy attack flying viruses and stop them from touching the server at the bottom of the screen. If you successfully block 30 viruses, you win the game!

Let's start by opening the blank project **04 – Hack Attack!.sb2** (File ▶ Upload from your computer). I used a sparkly photo of Hong Kong's skyline as my Stage. You can use whatever you like!

Did you know you can add programs to the Stage, too? We can add this program to make our city glow!

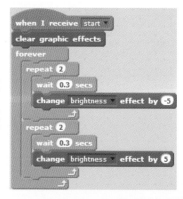

```
when I receive start
clear graphic effects
forever
  repeat 2
    wait 0.3 secs
    change brightness effect by -5
  repeat 2
    wait 0.3 secs
    change brightness effect by 5
```

Now let's take a look at the **Instructions** sprite. It tells the player how the game works. We'll write two programs to control it.

Protect Hong Kong!
Defend the server from virus attacks

Click your mouse to move Scratchy!
Press <SPACE> to start!

❶
```
when       clicked
go to x: 0 y: 0
show
forever
    if     key space ▾ pressed?   then
        broadcast space ▾
        hide
```

❷
```
when I receive space ▾
broadcast start ▾
```

Program ❶ makes the sprite show up at the start of the game and disappear when the player presses space, the spacebar on their keyboard.

Program ❷ makes the Instructions sprite broadcast start when it receives the space broadcast from program ❶. This will start the game!

Scripts Costumes Sounds

New costume:

Neo-cat2

1

Neo-cat1
90x111

2

Neo-cat2
150x117

Next, let's write some programs for Scratchy. Notice that he has two costumes already: one where he's just standing and another where he's jumping.

So let's add some programs to control how Scratchy looks. In program **1**, we **hide** him before the start broadcast is received. In program **2**, we control how Scratchy switches costumes. Whenever the player's mouse is clicked—that is, whenever **mouse down?**—Scratchy looks like he's jumping.

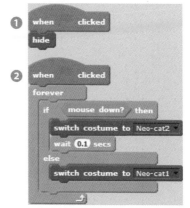

③
```
when I receive start ▼
go to x: -185 y: -115
point in direction 90▼
go to front
show
forever
    if    mouse down?   then
        point towards mouse-pointer ▼
        glide 0.1 secs to x: mouse x y: mouse y
```

④
```
when I receive Oh ▼
say OH NO!! for 0.3 secs
```

But how does the player control Scratchy? Program ③ lets you control Scratchy with the mouse, showing him only when the start broadcast is received.

Program ④ makes a speech bubble saying "OH NO!!" appear whenever the Scratchy sprite receives the Oh signal. We'll broadcast Oh whenever a virus manages to hit the server.

Tip: By using the mouse instead of the keyboard, the player has a lot of control over Scratchy, who will move very quickly for this game. But remember—every game is different! Sometimes the keyboard works well, too.

Time to program a new sprite! Switch to the **Server**. It should look like the image below, but we want it centered and at the bottom of the screen. Add this simple program so that the Server appears in the correct place.

Next, we'll program our computer opponent! The sprite called **Virus** has a set of costumes of letters spelling V–I–R–U–S.

Program ❶ hides the Virus until the game starts. Program ❷ makes the Virus switch costumes as it flies around.

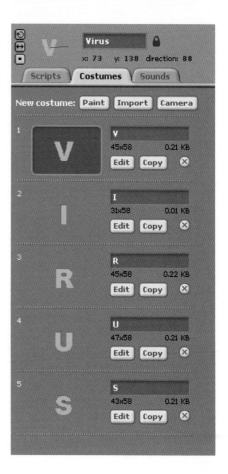

Program ❸ for the Virus makes it fly around. It bounces whenever it bumps into Scratchy or the edges of the screen.

Now we'll add more programs to the Virus to keep score. These programs use blocks from the **Control**, **Events**, and **Data** palettes to record and signal the conditions for winning and losing.

Program ❹ creates a new variable called score and the conditions we need to meet for the script to broadcast win. Your score will now appear on the Stage.

❹

```
when I receive start ▼
set score ▼ to 0
wait 0.5 secs
forever
    if        touching Neo-cat ▼ ?   then
        change score ▼ by 1
        wait 0.5 secs
    if     score > 29   then
        hide
        broadcast win ▼ and wait
        stop all ▼
```

❺

Program ❺ creates a variable called chance, which keeps track of how many times the Virus is allowed to touch the Server sprite before the player loses. We'll give Scratchy five chances to start. When you're out of chances, the program broadcasts lose. Just like the player's score, the number of tries the player has left is displayed on the Stage as chance.

```
when I receive start ▼
set chance ▼ to 5
wait 0.5 secs
forever
    if        touching Server ▼ ?   then
        change chance ▼ by -1
        broadcast Oh ▼
        wait 0.5 secs
    if     chance < 1   then
        hide
        broadcast lose ▼ and wait
```

Tip: When setting the rules for winning and losing in your games, use the greater-than symbol (>) or the less-than symbol (<) instead of the equal sign (=) , as we do in programs ❹ and ❺. This will prevent the game from breaking when a variable changes too quickly!

Why might the variable change too fast in this game? Scratchy might touch the Virus a few times in quick succession, and the program won't realize that you've won the game.

Now let's look at the sprite for the winning screen. Programs ❶ and ❷ keep it hidden. Then program ❸ makes it appear when the win broadcast is received from the Virus sprite.

You Win!!
The city server is safe now!

The losing screen is pretty similar to the winning screen. To save time, we can select the **Duplicate** tool and click the winning screen to copy both the image and the programming!

All we need to do now is change the costume and the last program a bit.

You Lose!!
Press <SPACE> to try again!

We're finished! After you save the file, hurry and help Scratchy the hacker defend the network from the virus attack!

Scratchy's Challenge!!

How would you make this game harder for the player? How about adding different kinds of viruses? What about turning this game into a two-player Ping-Pong match? Give it a try!

PENALTY KICK IN IPANEMA

STAGE 5

ACCORDING TO THE SECRET MANUAL, THE VIRUS CAME FROM IPANEMA!

THAT'S THE FAMOUS IPANEMA BEACH IN RIO DE JANEIRO, BRAZIL!

EEK! DO I HAVE TO WEAR A SWIMSUIT?

RIO DE JANEIRO

I CAN FEEL A COSMIC DEFENDER NEARBY!

WOW...BUT EVERYONE'S FROZEN!

NOT EVERYONE... I CAN HEAR A SQUEAKING NOISE FROM FAR AWAY!

GOBO! FABU! I'M TRAPPED IN THIS GOALPOST!

HANG IN THERE, PELE... WHAT ARE WE GOING TO DO?

IF YOU WANT TO BEAT A GOALPOST, THEN YOU'LL HAVE TO USE A SOCCER BALL!

LET ME TAKE ON THE CHALLENGE THIS TIME!

RIO SHOOT-OUT

Chapter Focus

Learn how to program a soccer game with a targeting system, several related rules, interactive sound effects, and a vivid, animated backdrop!

The Game

Shoot penalty kicks and avoid the moving goalie. You'll win the game if you manage to score five out of eight tries!

Bull's-eye

Here's a look at the final game. We'll need to create a targeting system that will move over the goal. When you press the spacebar, you'll kick the ball where the bull's-eye is. But watch out—the goalkeeper will dive every time you kick the ball!

To start, you can upload the file **05 – Rio Shootout.sb2** (File ▶ Upload from your computer), which has all our sprites but no programming blocks yet.

You can draw your very own backdrop if you like!

STAGE 5

Cloud | Clear

```
when [ ] clicked
go to x: 20 y: 30
forever
  repeat 2
    wait 0.4 secs
    change y by -1
  repeat 2
    wait 0.4 secs
    change y by 1
```

I created a sprite for the clouds. Click the **Cloud** sprite, and then add a program to make it float up and down. This will make the backdrop livelier!

Scripts | Costumes | Sounds

New costume:

Cloud

1

Cloud
233x37

If there's a beach, there must be some waves! The **Wave** sprite is separate from the background, and we'll give it some programs of its own.

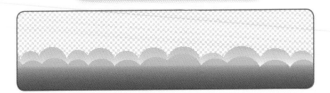

74

Since waves move up and down as well, their programming will be similar to the script for the clouds. Here's a little trick: First, select your Cloud sprite from the Sprite List, and drag its program to the picture icon of the Wave sprite in the Sprite List. Make sure your cursor is right over the Wave in the Sprite List, and then release your mouse. Now you've copied the programming for the Cloud sprite to the Wave sprite!

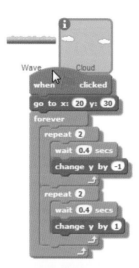

We can also change the Wave's script to make it move faster and more frequently than our clouds.

Then we can switch to our **Goalpost** sprite and write a program to set its position in the center of the field.

75

The goal's **Net** has its own sprite. Click it in the Sprite List, and then create this short program to set its position.

Now is a good time to test your program to make sure everything appears where you want it to. Try clicking ⚑. If your clouds float, the waves lap against the beach, and your goal and net are in the right place, let's move on to programming the game itself.

Next we'll program the **Bullseye** sprite, which shows where Mitch will kick the ball.

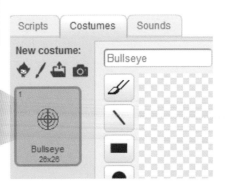

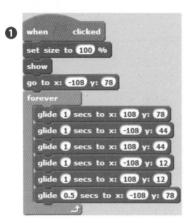

1 Program **1** will make the bull's-eye zigzag across the goal.

2 For program **2**, add these two set commands from the **Data** palette in a forever loop. We'll use these variables to determine where the ball goes after Mitch kicks it. You'll need to create X and Y in the **Data** palette.

Tip: Since our player doesn't need this information, we can hide the variables from being displayed on the screen by deselecting them in the **Data** palette.

3

4 Then add in programs **3** and **4** to the Bullseye sprite. Program **3** makes the bull's-eye continuously change color. Program **4** makes the bull's-eye disappear when it receives the shoot broadcast. Now when Mitch kicks the ball, the bull's-eye will disappear.

To make this game even more fun, we gave Pele the Keeper two costumes. That means we can program a simple animation by switching costumes.

Scripts | Costumes | Sounds

New costume:

Keeper

1
Keeper
180x154

2
Keeper1
180x154

We'll write two programs for Pele. Program ❶ sets his size, costume, and starting position and then animates him using the `next costume` command in a `forever` loop.

When he receives the Shoot broadcast in program ❷, he'll "dive" to a random spot in the goal to try to stop the ball! The `pick random` blocks are in the **Operators** palette—just drag two right into the `glide` block.

❶
```
when      clicked
set size to 45 %
switch costume to Keeper1
go to x: 0 y: 20
forever
    wait 0.5 secs
    next costume
```

❷
```
when I receive Shoot
glide 0.5 secs to x: pick random -90 to 90 y: pick random 20 to 70
wait 2 secs
go to x: 0 y: 20
```

Now we'll move on to program the game's most important feature—the ball.

| Scripts | Costumes | Sounds |

New costume:

Ball

Ball
80x80

New sound:

1 Whistle
00:00.2

2 Kickoff
00:00.4

3 Goal
00:01.5

4 Boo
00:00.9

First, click the **Ball** in the Sprite List. Check out all the different sound effects I've added in the **Sounds** tab. You can also use your own custom sounds!

Next, write program ❶ to set its starting position and size, and then play the Whistle sound.

Tip: The first two blocks (go to front and go back 1 layers) adjust the layer value so the Ball will appear in front of the Net, Stage, and other sprites in the game.

❶ when clicked
go to front
go back ❶ layers
set size to 50 %
go to x: 0 y: -80
play sound Whistle until done

By creating variables for Ball and Score, you can keep track of how many times the player has kicked the ball and how many times he has scored a point. Program ❷ sets the starting values for these variables.

Program ❸ will broadcast Shoot whenever the spacebar is pressed. Notice how there's an **if** loop that uses a **not** block from the **Operators** palette to make sure the player isn't out of balls (Ball > 0) and hasn't won the game (Score = 5).

Program ❹ is a neat animation trick. It makes the ball shrink into the distance by using a negative value (-2) in the **change size by** block.

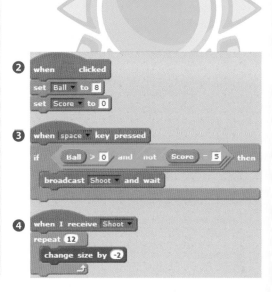

Program ❺ is quite special. First, it makes the ball **glide to** our variables X and Y. (Just drag them from the **Data** palette right into the **glide** block.) The two **if** loops contain the game's program for scoring. It broadcasts either Goal or Miss, depending on whether or not the ball touches Pele.

You'll score a goal if you manage to sneak the ball by our goalkeeper Pele!

6 when I receive Goal ▼
change Score ▼ by **1**
say GOAL!! for **1** secs
wait **1** secs
set size to **50** %
go to x: **0** y: **-80**

7 when I receive Miss ▼
change Score ▼ by **0**
say Miss!! for **1** secs
wait **1** secs
set size to **50** %
go to x: **0** y: **-80**

Now let's add some more programs to the Ball. In programs **6** and **7**, we'll determine what happens after a Goal or Miss. Program **6** will change the Score by 1, while program **7** will change it by 0. Whether the player scores or not, the ball returns to its original position after 1 second.

8 when I receive Shoot ▼
play sound Kickoff ▼ until done

9 when I receive Goal ▼
play sound Goal ▼ until done

10 when I receive Miss ▼
play sound Boo ▼ until done

Programs **8**, **9**, and **10** play sound effects for fun.

11 when I receive Goal ▼
wait **1** secs
if (Score = **5**) then
    broadcast Won ▼ and wait

12 when I receive Goal ▼
wait **1** secs
if (Ball = **0** and not (Score = **5**)) then
    broadcast Lost ▼ and wait

13 when I receive Miss ▼
wait **1** secs
if (Ball = **0**) then
    broadcast Lost ▼ and wait

Next, we set the rules for winning and losing the game. Program **11** will broadcast Won when the Score variable reaches 5. Programs **12** and **13** will broadcast Lose after all the player's chances are up; that is, when Ball = 0. (Without program **13**, the player can still lose even if he scores with his last ball.)

Finally, it's time to program our **Banner** sprite. It has three costumes for the game instructions (Start), the winning screen (Won), and the losing screen (Lost).

Score 5 to win!!

You Won!!

You Lost!!

Then we add these three programs to show the costumes at the right time. Script ❶ shows the Start costume so the player has instructions at the start of the game. The Won broadcast will make costume Won appear in script ❷, and the same happens for the Lost costume and Lost broadcast in script ❸. The `stop all` block at the end of scripts ❷ and ❸ will stop the game.

❶
```
when       clicked
go to x: 0 y: -40
go to front
switch costume to Start
show
wait 0.5 secs
hide
```

❷
```
when I receive Won
go to x: 0 y: -55
switch costume to Won
show
stop all
```

❸
```
when I receive Lost
go to x: 0 y: -55
switch costume to Lost
show
stop all
```

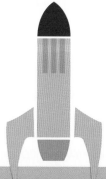

Don't forget to save your game before you take on the challenge to show off your soccer skills! Remember: Press the spacebar to kick the ball.

Scratchy's Challenge!!

Can you transform this into a shooting gallery game at an amusement park? How about making Pele a better goalkeeper? Give it a try!

SCRATCHY'S WILD RIDE

GOAL!!!

THE LOCK IS BROKEN! WHAT AWESOME SOCCER SKILLS!

BAM!

WELL... I ONLY WON BECAUSE OF EVERYONE'S HELP AND THE DIRECTIONS FROM THE SECRET MANUAL!

DON'T SELL YOURSELF SHORT, MITCH!

PELE'S BACK! ALL THE COSMIC DEFENDERS ARE BACK TOGETHER AGAIN!

LET'S WORK TOGETHER TO RESTORE THE BALANCE OF THE UNIVERSE!

THERE'S A MAGIC GEM IN THE GREAT PYRAMID OF GIZA. WE NEED TO GET IT BEFORE THE DARK WIZARD DOES!

OH NO! WE CAN'T OPEN A STARGATE NEAR THE PYRAMID BECAUSE OF THE MAGIC GEM'S INFLUENCE!

I GUESS WE'LL HAVE TO GET THERE THE OLD-FASHIONED WAY!

THE SAHARA DESERT

THE TRUCK'S READY TO GO. HOP ON, EVERYBODY!

HOLD ON TIGHT!

AHHH!

NO!! THEY TOOK MITCH!

HURRY UP AND START THE CAR! WE HAVE TO CATCH THEM!

DESERT RALLY RACE

STAGE 6

✚ Chapter Focus

Learn how to create a scrolling game, program complex movements for the sprites, and make a backdrop change over time.

✐ Game

Control Scratchy's car to avoid obstacles and to run away from the Dark Minions in order to reach the Great Pyramid of Giza. Each time you crash your car, one of the Cosmic Defenders will jump out. If you crash your car four times, your car will break down!

Let's start by uploading a project called **06 – Desert Rally.sb2** (File ▸ Upload from your computer), which already has a bunch of sprites in it. It doesn't have any programs yet, but we'll add some soon.

First, let's look at the Stage. If you click the **Stage** in the Sprite List, you can see that we have a lot of different backdrops.

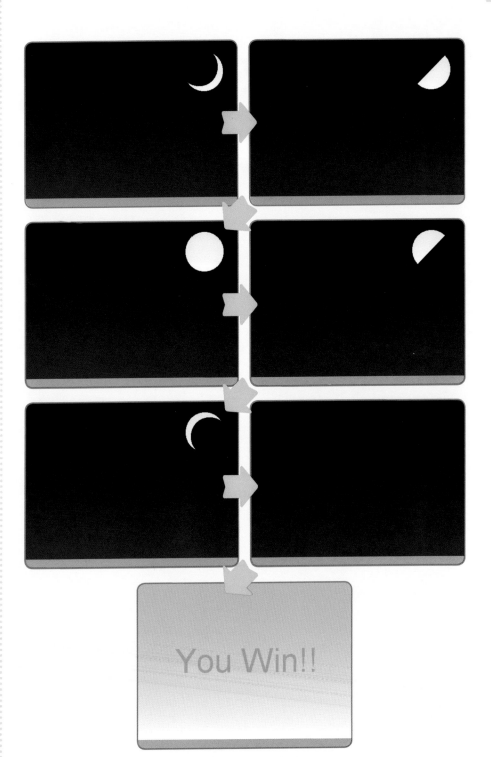

You Win!!

Backdrops for the Stage are just like costumes for any other kind of sprite. So let's write a program that controls how they change.

Program ❶ will make the backdrop change over time in two loops, day and night. You can use the Duplicate tool to save time with the programming! This animation will give the Stage a cool look as Scratchy drives.

Program ❷ will make the Stage change its backdrop to the Win costume when the finish broadcast is received.

❶
```
when [ ] clicked
forever
    repeat 8
        switch backdrop to Day_1
        wait 0.5 secs
        switch backdrop to Day_2
        wait 0.5 secs
        switch backdrop to Day_3
        wait 0.5 secs
        switch backdrop to Day_4
        wait 0.5 secs
    repeat 4
        switch backdrop to Night_1
        wait 0.5 secs
        switch backdrop to Night_2
        wait 0.5 secs
        switch backdrop to Night_3
        wait 0.5 secs
        switch backdrop to Night_4
        wait 0.5 secs
        switch backdrop to Night_5
        wait 0.5 secs
        switch backdrop to Night_6
        wait 0.5 secs
```

❷
```
when I receive finish
switch backdrop to Win
stop all
```

We'll also have the Stage keep track of the time in program ❸. So create a variable called Time from the **Data** palette. We set Time to 0 and then change it by 1 with each second. We'll use the Time variable again later.

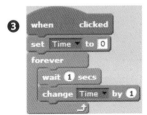

Next, let's look at the road. Try to use the whole width of the Stage if you're drawing it!

Adding these programs to the **Road1** sprite will make it appear on the screen and scroll to the left.

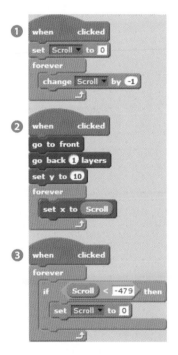

1
```
when [🏳] clicked
set Scroll to 0
forever
    change Scroll by -1
```

Write program **1** to make the Scroll variable continuously decrease by 1 (that is, `change Scroll by -1`).

2
```
when [🏳] clicked
go to front
go back 1 layers
set y to 10
forever
    set x to Scroll
```

Program **2** will set the road's position. Set the y coordinate to 10 so it won't move up or down, and then add `set x to Scroll` in a `forever` loop. By doing this, the road will continuously move to the left as the Scroll variable changes.

3
```
when [🏳] clicked
forever
    if < Scroll < -479 > then
        set Scroll to 0
```

Program **3** will make the Scroll variable reset to a 0 value once it reaches a value less than −479.

Tip: Why did we use the number −479? The width of the entire Scratch Stage is 480 pixels, so that's when it will roll off the Stage.

Now duplicate the Road1 sprite to create a second sprite called **Road2**.

Add this program to use the Scroll variable from the first road sprite. This time, we use a trick to make Road2 follow right behind Road1. By setting the x coordinate to Scroll + 480, we know Road2 will always follow behind Road1. This means that the player always has a road to drive on, no matter what!

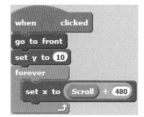

Next, switch to Scratchy's **Car** sprite.

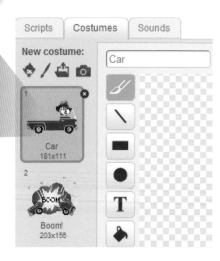

Program ➊ for the Car does a lot of work. First, it sets the costume, size, and position.

The forever loop holds the rest of the program. The change y by -5 block will pull the car down, giving it gravity. The if touching color block makes the car bounce up whenever it touches the black part of the road, making it seem like they're driving on a very bumpy road. The if key up arrow pressed? block will broadcast jump and then wait.

➊
```
when      clicked
switch costume to Car ▼
set size to 60 %
go to front
go to x: -150 y: -105
forever
    change y by -5
    if   touching color ■ ?  and  y position < -105  then
        change y by 10
        wait 0.05 secs

    if   key up arrow ▼ pressed?  then
        broadcast jump ▼ and wait
```

➋
```
when I receive jump ▼
repeat 15
    change y by 12
repeat until  touching color ■ ?  and  y position < -105
    change y by -5
```

Program ➋ makes the car "listen" for the jump broadcast and makes the car jump up.

The broadcast jump and wait block in program ➊ will temporarily stop the first program so the second program can run.

Now add program **3** so that the car can move left and right.

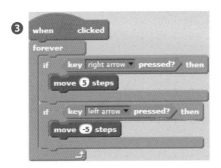

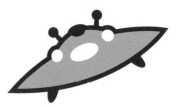

In program **4**, we add some speech bubbles as instructions for the player.

In program **5**, we create a new variable called Life. When the Life value is less than 1, we'll set the car's costume to Boom! and then end the game with the `stop all` command.

4
```
when     clicked
say  Press L or R keys to move, UP key to jump!  for  2  secs
say  Avoid the obstacles!  for  2  secs
```

5
```
when     clicked
set  Life  to  4
wait  1  secs
forever
    if  Life < 1  then
        switch costume to  Boom!
        stop  all
```

Once you're finished with the Car sprite's programming, you can add some passengers—the Cosmic Defenders!

You can use the three sprites that are already in the project, or draw your own. I put **Gobo** at the back, **Fabu** in the middle, and **Pele** in the front. It's okay if your sprites overlap a bit—these guys are just coming along for the ride.

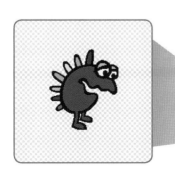

Scripts | Costumes | Sounds

New costume:

Gobo

Gobo
104x120

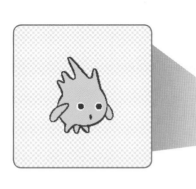

Scripts | Costumes | Sounds

New costume:

Fabu

Fabu
112x126

Scripts | Costumes | Sounds

New costume:

Pele

Pele
116x144

Write this program for Gobo. It sets his size and position and uses the `go to` block so he'll always follow the Car sprite. Once the variable Life drops to less than 4 (`Life < 4`), he'll shoot to a random area. When he touches the top of the screen (`y position = 180`), we make him disappear by using the `hide` block.

```
when        clicked
set size to  30  %
go to front
go back  1  layers
show
point in direction  90▾
go to  Car ▾
forever
    repeat until   Life  <  4
        change y by  10
        wait  0.05  secs
        go to  Car ▾

    point in direction  pick random  15  to  345
    glide  1  secs to x:  pick random  250  to  -250   y:  180
    if    y position  =  180   then
        hide

    hide
```

x: -149
y: -105

```
when clicked
set size to 30 %
go to front
go back 2 layers
show
point in direction 90▾
go to Car ▾
forever
    repeat until ( Life < 3 )
        change y by 10
        wait 0.05 secs
        go to Car ▾
    point in direction ( pick random 15 to 345 )
    glide 1 secs to x: ( pick random 250 to -250 ) y: 180
    if ( y position = 180 ) then
        hide
    hide
```

x: -149
y: -105

Drag and copy Gobo's program onto Fabu in the Sprite List. You'll need to change only a few things. Most important, change the `repeat until` block to `Life < 3`, so Fabu will bounce out at a different time.

```
when clicked
set size to 25 %
go to front
go back 3 layers
show
point in direction 90▾
go to Car ▾
forever
    repeat until ( Life < 2 )
        change y by 10
        wait 0.05 secs
        go to Car ▾
    point in direction ( pick random 15 to 345 )
    glide 1 secs to x: ( pick random 250 to -250 ) y: 180
    if ( y position = 180 ) then
        hide
    hide
```

x: -149
y: -105

Do the same thing for Pele, but change the Life value to 2. Because Pele's sprite is a little bigger than the others, we also set his size to 25%.

Now we can add the programming for the obstacles. First, let's take a look at the thorny and dangerous **Bush** sprite! It has two costumes.

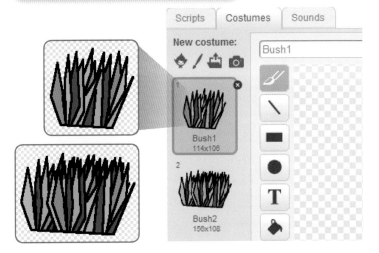

Scripts | Costumes | Sounds

New costume:

Bush1

1 Bush1 114x106

2 Bush2 156x108

And then write these three programs:

Program ❶ controls when the bush appears and makes sure it moves with the road. Once it touches the left edge of the screen, it'll disappear and switch to the next bush costume.

Program ❷ programs the Car to change Life by -1 (that is, lose one life) whenever it touches an obstacle. Notice how we programmed the computer to check if the player still has enough Life value left using the and and not blocks.

And program ❸ makes the bush disappear once it receives the finish signal, which ends the game.

❶
```
when clicked
switch costume to Bush1
hide
forever
    wait 8 secs
    go to x: 230 y: -130
    show
    repeat until  x position < -230
        change x by -1
    hide
    next costume
```

❷
```
when clicked
wait 1 secs
forever
    if  touching Car ?  and  not  Life = 0  then
        change Life by -1
        wait 6 secs
```

❸
```
when I receive finish
hide
```

Now let's look at the **Tower** sprite, which also has two costumes. This obstacle will be tough to jump!

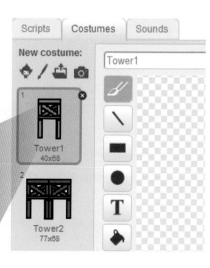

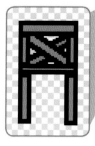

```
when [] clicked
switch costume to Tower1
hide
forever
    wait 18 secs
    go to x: 230 y: -130
    show
    repeat until  x position < -230
        change x by -1

    hide
    next costume


when [] clicked
wait 1 secs
forever
    if  touching Car ? and not  Life = 0  then
        change Life by -1
        wait 6 secs



when I receive finish
hide
```

We can once again copy the program we created for the bushes. Edit the costume name and the time it appears, and you're good to go!

Take a look at the sprite for **Legs**, the evil octopus Dark Minion. But don't you think it's a little boring just to have one image for him?

Why don't we try animating him?

In the Paint Editor, use the **Select** tool to grab the end of his tentacle.

Next, click this button to flip his arm up and then drag it back into place.

Do the same for his other tentacles, and there you go—a new look!

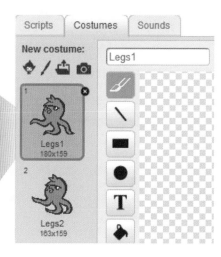

Tip: Editing existing costumes is an easy way to animate a character without having to redraw it. The Select and Rotate tools let you quickly change the position of a sprite's arms and legs.

Vector-based art is even easier to squish and squeeze into new shapes—this makes it great for animating characters.

Now let's get back to programming! Program ❶ makes Legs switch between his two costumes in a forever loop. Program ❷ makes him hide when he receives the finish broadcast.

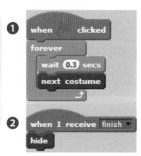

Programs ❸ and ❹ control Legs's movements and make him an unpredictable obstacle for Scratchy's car.

❸
```
when [ ] clicked
set size to 50 %
hide
forever
    wait pick random 15 to 20 secs
    go to x: 230 y: 70
    show
    repeat until ( x position < -230 )
        change x by -3
    hide
```

❹
```
when [ ] clicked
forever
    repeat 10
        change y by -5
        wait 0.05 secs
    repeat 10
        change y by 5
        wait 0.05 secs
```

Lastly, program ❺ for Legs adds a condition that will subtract life points from the Life variable, just as with the Bush and Tower obstacles.

❺
```
when [ ] clicked
wait 1 secs
forever
    if < touching Car ? and not ( Life = 0 ) > then
        change Life by -1
        wait 6 secs
```

And now we'll move on to the final sprite of the game: Egypt's Great Pyramid of Giza! Let's start with this photo:

By using this sprite, we'll make it look like Scratchy is "arriving" at the pyramids. I edited the Giza costume so that the cool backdrops will show through and so that the bottom matches the orange of the road. Now we can make the photo fit into our existing game.

Write a script so that the pyramid slowly appears from the right, after the game is run for 60 seconds. Once it reaches the center of the screen (x position = 0), it broadcasts the finish signal. When the other sprites receive this signal, the game ends.

After saving your file, board Scratchy's speedy car and drive into the Sahara Desert to begin your wild adventure!

Scratchy's Challenge!!

Can you use these programs to create another scrolling game? Give it try! (Tip: The height of Scratch's screen is 360 pixels.) Make the game even more challenging by having the car go really fast!

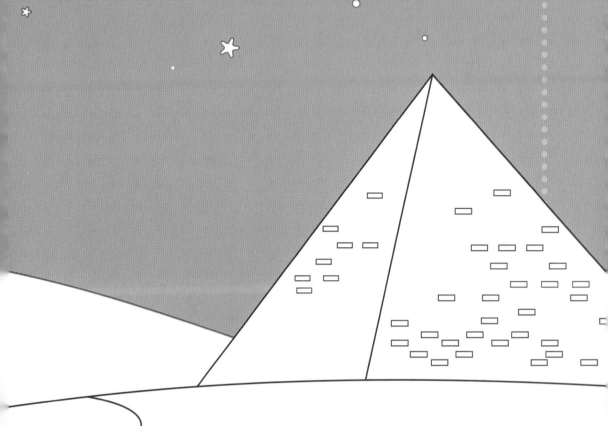

THE LOST TREASURES OF GIZA

THERE'S THE GREAT PYRAMID OF GIZA!

SNIFF WE TRIED OUR BEST, BUT THEY STILL GOT AWAY!

WHAT WILL WE DO WITHOUT MITCH'S PROGRAMMING?

DON'T GIVE UP! THERE HAS TO BE A WAY!

WE CAN TEACH SCRATCHY HOW TO USE THE SECRET MANUAL!

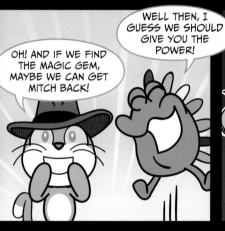

OH! AND IF WE FIND THE MAGIC GEM, MAYBE WE CAN GET MITCH BACK!

WELL THEN, I GUESS WE SHOULD GIVE YOU THE POWER!

BZZT BZZT

THANKS, GUYS! I KNOW HOW TO USE IT NOW!

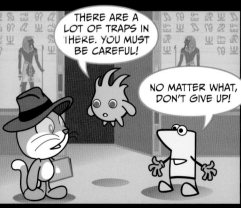

THERE ARE A LOT OF TRAPS IN THERE. YOU MUST BE CAREFUL!

NO MATTER WHAT, DON'T GIVE UP!

SIGH AND I THOUGHT EGYPTIANS LIKED CATS.

ESCAPE THE MAZE!

✚ Chapter Focus

Learn how to design an interactive maze with a guard, booby traps, and treasure!

✏ Game

Guide Scratchy through the maze, and into the treasure room to collect the Magic Gem. After he picks up the Magic Gem, other traps in the pyramid are sprung, and he must escape!

For this game, begin by uploading a project file called **07 – The Maze.sb2** (File ▶ Upload from your computer). This project file has all the images you need for the game, but none of the sprites have any programs yet.

Take a look around, and especially take notice of the Stage. You can see that all of the walls in our maze have the same orange color. We'll use that color as the boundary, so Scratchy can't walk through walls!

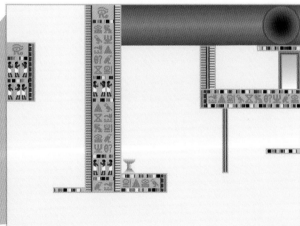

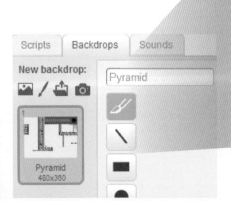

Click the sprite for Scratchy called **Indy-Cat** in the Sprite List. Then click the **Sounds** tab and add a sound effect for him. Either record a "meow" yourself or use the **Cat** sound effect. We'll write a program to make Scratchy meow whenever he bumps into a bad guy or trap.

Let's begin by thinking about how the game should start and how the player will win at the end of the game.

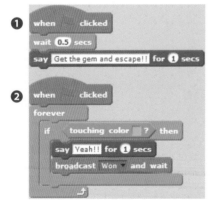

Program **1** gives the player the instructions for the game using the say block. Now when the game starts, the player will know he needs to grab the Magic Gem to win.

And, of course, to end the game, Scratchy needs to escape the maze with the Magic Gem. Now let's write a program for the end of the game. Program **2** uses a special kind of block within a forever if loop. If Scratchy touches the color blue—that is, the blue sky of the exit door—he'll say "Yeah!!" and broadcast Won, which will cause the game to end. (Because the maze itself doesn't have any blue, we don't have to worry about ending the game accidentally.)

To write program **2**, drag the touching color command from the **Sensing** palette into the if block. Click the color inside the block, and an eyedropper appears. Click the blue of the doorway, and you're all set. We'll use the touching color command for another neat programming trick next.

Now take a look at program ❸. It looks pretty complicated, but it's really not so hard. Can you tell what it does just by reading it?

❸
```
when      clicked
point in direction 90▾
go to x: -205 y: 150
go to front
go back 1 layers
forever
  if      key up arrow ▾ pressed?   then
    change y by 3
    if      touching color    ?   then
      change y by -3

  if      key down arrow ▾ pressed?   then
    change y by -3
    if      touching color    ?   then
      change y by 3

  if      key left arrow ▾ pressed?   then
    point in direction -90▾
    change x by -3
    if      touching color    ?   then
      change x by 3

  if      key right arrow ▾ pressed?   then
    point in direction 90▾
    change x by 3
    if      touching color    ?   then
      change x by -3
```

First, we set the direction and position of Scratchy. That's simple enough. But what about the big forever loop? That holds all of the rest of the program, and that's how we'll program Scratchy's movements. First, if you press the up key, you can see there's a command that will change y by 3. But then *inside* that if loop, there's a second if loop!

If Scratchy is touching orange, the computer tells Scratchy to change y by -3. What's that all about? Well, did you notice that the walls of the maze are all orange? So if Scratchy bumps into the orange wall, we want the wall to stop him. And what does 3 + (-3) equal? That's right, 0. So when Scratchy touches the orange wall, he doesn't change his y position at all. He won't move! Cool.

The down, left, and right if loops work in just the same way, and they have a second if loop inside them as well. Make sure to pick orange with the eyedropper for every if touching color command.

Now Scratchy can't walk through the maze's walls or gates. Notice that the edge of the Stage has a thin band of orange, too. Scratchy can't walk off the Stage either! He's trapped in our maze, just like we want.

Finally, for program ❹, we use the forever if block and the or block to program what will happen whenever Scratchy bumps into a trap or a bad guy. A speech bubble will say "Oh!", the sound effect Cat will play, and Scratchy returns to his starting position.

Tip: The second say block is blank. This makes the "Oh!" disappear.

❹
```
when      clicked
wait 1 secs
forever
  if   touching Turnstile ▾ ? or touching Whiptail ▾ ? or touching Wall_L ▾ ? or touching Wall_R ▾ ? or touching Stone ▾ ?   then
    say Oh!
    play sound Cat ▾
    glide 1 secs to x: -205 y: 150
    say
```

Now is a good time to make sure that your programs work as you expected. Click 🏴, and make sure Scratchy moves up, down, left, and right. Try bumping into the walls of the maze. Does Scratchy stop moving once he hits a wall in all four directions? If not, go back and double-check your programming. (Remember that if Scratchy touches the orange wall, his movement should add up to 0.) Try hitting an obstacle or a bad guy to make sure Scratchy returns to the start of the maze.

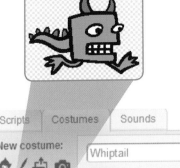

Next, click the sprite for **Whiptail**, the Dark Minion guarding the pyramid. Write a program that sets his size and starting position and then makes him pace back and forth in the maze.

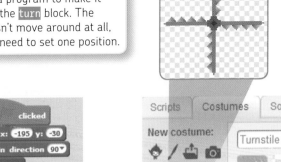

Then click the **Turnstile** sprite, and write a program to make it spin using the turn block. The sprite doesn't move around at all, so we just need to set one position.

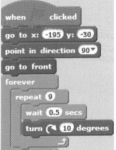

At this point, take a look at the **Lock** and **Key** sprites, which are circled in blue below. Scratchy will need to pick up the Key first, in order to open the Lock. Let's create some programs for them next.

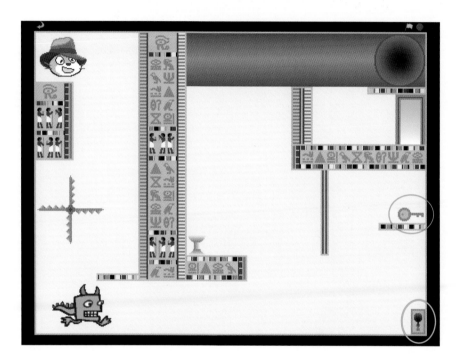

First, click the **Lock** in the Sprite List to give it a simple program—this just sets its location in the maze. The program that actually opens the gate is in the Key sprite.

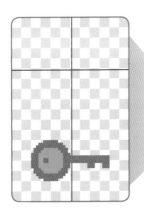

Tip: When creating the Key sprite, I used the **Set Costume Center** button in the Paint Editor to make sure Scratchy and the Key don't overlap.

Click the **Key** in the Sprite List, and listen to its sound in the **Sounds** tab. Then click the **Scripts** tab to write this program. We want a sound to play when Scratchy picks up the Key and then have the Key follow Scratchy, using the `go to` command. When the Key touches the Lock, the `Gate Open` signal is broadcast.

```
when  clicked
go to x: 220 y: 0
show
wait until  touching Indy-Cat ▾ ?
play sound AfroString ▾
forever
    go to Indy-Cat ▾
    if  touching Lock ▾ ? then
        play sound AfroString ▾
        broadcast Gate Open ▾
        hide
```

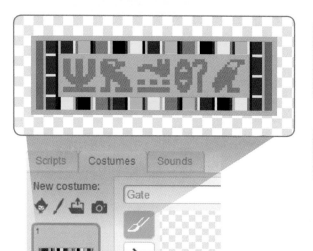

Now to program the **Gate** sprite. Because it has an orange border just like our maze, Scratchy can't enter the treasure room unless it moves!

Click the **Gate** in the Sprite List, and then test out the DirtyWhir sound to the Gate in its **Sounds** tab.

Now for some programs. Program ❶ just sets the Gate's location. Program ❷ makes the Gate glide out of the way when the Gate Open broadcast signal is received. Program ❸ plays a sound effect.

If you haven't tried out the game yet, give it a test now by clicking ⚑! See if you can get Scratchy to enter the treasure room.

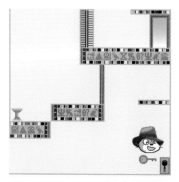

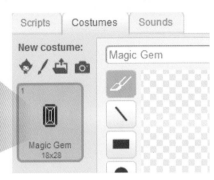

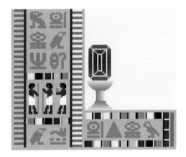

Next, let's program the **Magic Gem** sprite. We'll use a sound effect called Fairydust in the **Sounds** tab.

If it's not already there, you can just drag the sprite on top of its stand on the Stage.

❶
```
when       clicked
clear graphic effects
forever
    change color ▾ effect by 25
```

❷
```
when       clicked
go to x: -42 y: -48
show
wait until  touching Indy-Cat ▾ ?
play sound Fairydust ▾
think Gem Obtained!! for 1 secs
broadcast Stone ▾
hide
```

Then write two programs for it. Program ❶ makes the Magic Gem change colors. Program ❷ sets the Magic Gem's position and then uses a `wait until` block to determine what happens when Scratchy grabs the Magic Gem. When Scratchy touches the Magic Gem, it broadcasts Stone. This will release the final traps in the maze!

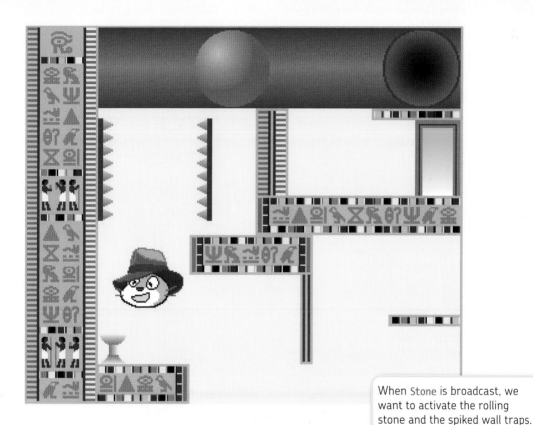

When Stone is broadcast, we want to activate the rolling stone and the spiked wall traps.

Our spiked wall trap will actually be two different sprites. **Wall_L** (the left side of the trap) gets one simple program to set its position.

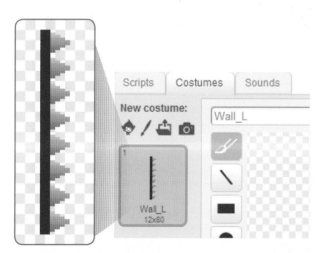

The right side has its own sprite called **Wall_R**. Create these two programs to set the position and make it move. This wall listens for the Stone broadcast and begins to glide back and forth, most dangerously!

Waiting outside the passage is a rolling boulder sprite called **Stone**. I've used different shades of gray for the Stone to give it a 3D look.

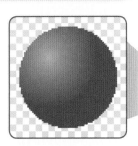

Program ❶ for the Stone will make the sprite appear to roll, giving it a realistic animation. Program ❷ controls the movement of the Stone—it rolls down the passage and then appears again at the start, in a forever loop.

Finally, we have a sprite for the winning screen called **Won**.

You Won!!

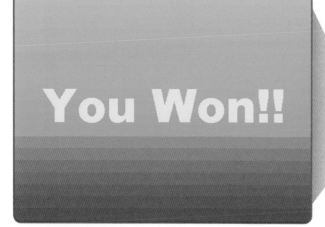

Write these three short programs. Program ❶ hides the sprite, and program ❷ displays it only when it receives Won. Program ❸ plays the sound effect we added in the **Sounds** tab.

Tip: The `stop all` command in program ❸ will make the Stone, Whiptail, and all other sprites stop moving.

Wondering where that Won broadcast will come from? Remember that Scratchy broadcasts Won when he touches the blue in the doorway. We added that way back in program ❷ on page 108. So we're finished! Yes!

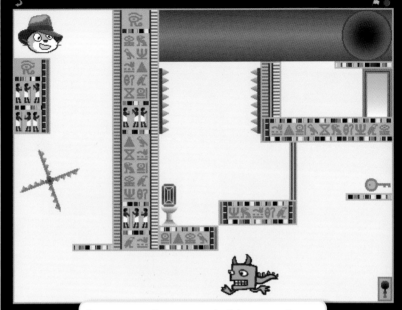

Save your project so you don't lose any of your work! Now help Scratchy collect the Magic Gem and escape from the dangerous maze.

Scratchy's Challenge!!

By making the sprites smaller, you can create an even more complicated maze with more traps. Or you could add a second player and make it a race to the finish! Give it a try!

WIZARD'S RACE!

SORCEROR'S CHALLENGE

+ Chapter Focus

Learn how to control the Stage with multiple costumes, play music with Scratch, and create other animations.

✏ The Game

This is a simple "button-mashing" game. Rapidly press two keys back and forth to make Scratchy fly. He needs to beat all three levels within 15 seconds to collect the second Magic Gem.

Open the Scratch project **08 – Wizard's Race.sb2** (File ▸ Upload from your computer). This project file has all the sprites you'll need, but it doesn't have any programs yet. We can customize how it looks later. For now, we'll focus on the programming.

First, let's take a look at the Stage. It has three backdrops. We'll use these as levels for Scratchy's ride on the broomstick.

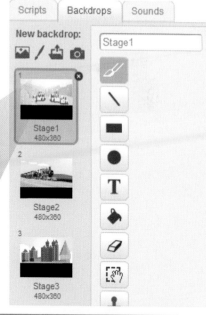

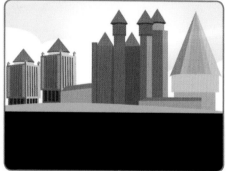

STAGE

1 Write program **1** for the Stage to set its first backdrop. Program **2** changes the Stage's backdrop when it receives the next level broadcast.

Tip: You'll need to choose **new message...** in the dropdown menu of the `when I receive` block to create the next level broadcast.

3 Create a LEVEL variable, and then write programs **3** and **4**. Program **3** makes sure that we start at level 1. Program **4** listens for the next level broadcast from program **4** on page 124 and increases the LEVEL variable by 1.

Create a second variable called TIME, and then write program **5**, which gives you 15 seconds to complete the race. Program **6** broadcasts LOSE when you've run out of time.

Tip: Program **6** has a couple tricky things in it. First, you'll need to create a new Start broadcast in the `when I receive` block. The script also makes use of Scratch's built-in timer variable and uses some special commands from the **Operators**, **Events**, **Sensing**, and **Data** palettes. You need to use the `reset timer` block in program **6**, as Scratch's timer starts just as soon as you open the project. This command will let you try the game again after you've lost, too.

Next, we'll program the sprite for Scratchy the wizard. The sprite is called **Harry-Catter** and has two costumes. We'll give him two sound effects, too, in the **Sounds** tab.

Scripts	Costumes	Sounds

New costume:

HarryCatter2

1

HarryCatter1
147x111

2

HarryCatter2
147x111

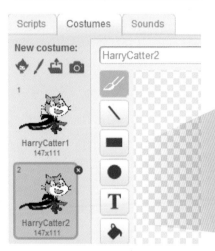

New sound:

1

Zoom
00:01.7

2

Fairydust
00:00.5

Then write program ❶ to set his starting costume and position. Program ❷ makes him float up and down.

❶
```
when clicked
go to x: -135 y: 65
switch costume to HarryCatter2
go to front
```

❷
```
when clicked
forever
    change y by 2
    wait 0.3 secs
    change y by -2
    wait 0.3 secs
```

Program ❸ controls how Scratchy moves. The player will need to press the left and right arrow keys, one after another, to move Scratchy.

❸

```
when I receive Start ▼
forever
    if   key left arrow ▼ pressed?  and  key right arrow ▼ pressed?  then
        move 0 steps

    if   key left arrow ▼ pressed?  and  not  key right arrow ▼ pressed?  then
        switch costume to HarryCatter1 ▼
        move 10 steps
        wait until  key right arrow ▼ pressed?  and  not  key left arrow ▼ pressed?
        switch costume to HarryCatter2 ▼
        move 10 steps
```

Can you see how this program works? The player can start with either the right or left arrow. The **not** block makes sure the player doesn't "cheat" by pressing both the right and left arrow keys at the same time.

❹

```
when I receive Start ▼
repeat 2
    wait until  touching Magic ▼ ?
    play sound Fairydust ▼
    play sound Zoom ▼
    broadcast next level ▼
    go to x: -135 y: 65
    say Next Level! for 0.5 secs

say Get the Magic Gem! for 1 secs
wait until  touching Magic ▼ ?
broadcast WIN ▼
```

Finally, write program ❹ so that once Scratchy reaches the **Magic** sprite, sound effects will play, next level is broadcast, and Scratchy says "Next Level!" Remember that the next level broadcast will make the Stage change backdrops.

After that loop repeats twice, the player is on the third level. Scratchy will now say "Get the Magic Gem!" and broadcast WIN if he reaches the Magic sprite in time.

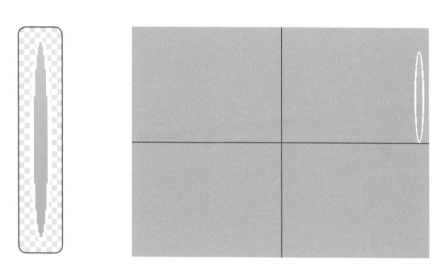

Now let's take a look at the costumes for Magic, the sprite that is our Magic Gate and the Magic Gem. The sprite will appear on the right of the Stage, and it will serve as Scratchy's goal for each of the three levels.

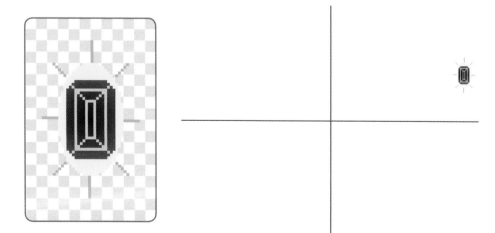

Costumes panel

New costume: Magic Gem1

1 — Magic Gate1
16x144

2 — Magic Gate2
16x144

3 — Magic Gem1
36x56

Here are those costumes for this sprite. We'll change costumes with each level, with the Magic Gem as Scratchy's goal for the third level. (That's why we have two Magic Gate costumes and one Magic Gem costume—we have three levels.)

❶
```
when   clicked
go to x: 0 y: 0
switch costume to Magic Gate1
forever
    change color effect by 10
```

❷
```
when I receive next level
next costume
```

❸
```
when   clicked
forever
    change y by 2
    wait 0.3 secs
    change y by -2
    wait 0.3 secs
```

Program ❶ sets the sprite's position and its first costume and creates a change color animation. Program ❷ changes the costume with each next level broadcast, and program ❸ makes the sprite float up and down.

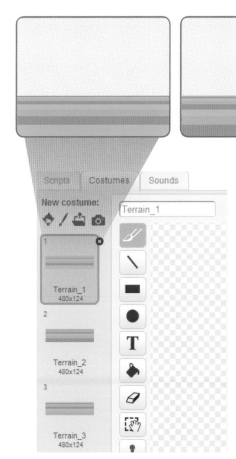

Now we can add some magical visual effects to our game. There is a sprite called **Terrain** that has these three costumes.

Next, write program ❶ to continuously change the Terrain sprite's costumes and set its starting position. This gives a neat animated effect to the ground. Program ❷ makes the Terrain change colors magically!

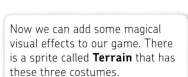

❶
```
when [green flag] clicked
go to x: 0 y: 0
switch costume to Terrain_1
forever
    wait 0.05 secs
    switch costume to Terrain_2
    wait 0.05 secs
    switch costume to Terrain_3
    wait 0.05 secs
    switch costume to Terrain_1
```

❷
```
when [green flag] clicked
forever
    change color effect by 1
```

Now it's time for the text for our game. The **Titles** sprite has a bunch of instructions for the player. We'll use its Countdown_3, Countdown_2, Countdown_1, and Go costumes to create a countdown to start this race!

New costume:

1

Instruction
467x89

2

Ready
264x88

3

Countdown_3
57x88

4

Countdown_2
57x88

5

Countdown_1
57x88

6

Go
173x88

7

Win
336x88

8

Lose
364x88

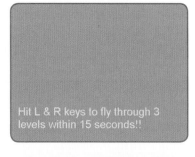

Hit L & R keys to fly through 3 levels within 15 seconds!!

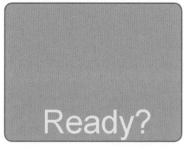

Ready?

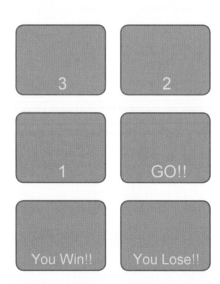

3

2

1

GO!!

You Win!!

You Lose!!

The Titles sprite has three sounds. You can add your own in the **Sounds** tab.

New sound:

1 Pop
00:00.0

2 WaterDrop
00:00.3

3 Xylo1
00:11.1

Write program ❶ to set the order of each costume. We use the `play note` and `play sound` blocks to add fun noises to the game.

❶
```
when     clicked
go to x: 0 y: 0
switch costume to Instruction
repeat 3
    play sound Pop
    show
    wait 0.4 secs
    hide
    wait 0.1 secs
switch costume to Ready
show
play sound WaterDrop until done
wait 0.5 secs
set instrument to 87
switch costume to Countdown_3
play note 60 for 0.8 beats
switch costume to Countdown_2
play note 60 for 0.8 beats
switch costume to Countdown_1
play note 60 for 0.8 beats
switch costume to Go
play note 72 for 0.8 beats
wait 0.5 secs
hide
broadcast Start
forever
    set volume to 50 %
    play sound Xylo1 until done
```

Here's that Start broadcast at long last. Remember that this is what the Stage and Scratchy are waiting for!

❷
```
when I receive WIN
switch costume to Win
show
stop all
```

❸
```
when I receive LOSE
switch costume to Lose
show
stop all
```

Finally, write programs ❷ and ❸ for the winning and losing screens, depending on whether the Titles sprite receives the WIN or LOSE broadcast. And now our game is complete!

TIME 15.0
LEVEL 1

Hit L & R keys to fly through 3 levels within 15 seconds!!

Save your project, and get ready for a race! Click 🏳, put your fingers on the keys, and get ready to set a speed record.

Scratchy's Challenge!!

Can you edit this game to make it a two-player race? How about a two-person watermelon-eating contest? Give it a try!

THE FINAL FIGHT... IN DARK SPACE

STAGE 9

THE FINAL FIGHT

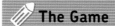

➕ Chapter Focus

Learn how to design a *fighting game*. We'll create two characters with unique fight moves, custom health counters, and more. To make custom animations for Scratchy's three fight moves, we'll use a special trick to swap between four different sprites.

✏️ The Game

Take control of Scratchy for the final fight with the Dark Wizard. Use his saber spin, saber throw, and force attack to defeat the Dark Wizard.

Here's a look at the final game we'll create. You'll need to jump over the Dark Wizard's dangerous fireballs and launch a counterattack!

This sprite represents the Dark Wizard's health.

This sprite represents Scratchy's health.

The computer controls the Dark Wizard.

The player controls Scratchy.

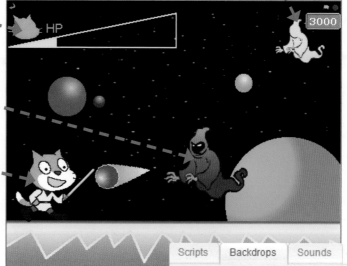

Let's start by uploading a blank project called **09 – Final Fight.sb2** (File ▶ Upload from your computer). This project has all the sprites we'll need, even the Stage. Now let's move on to the exciting stuff—programming!

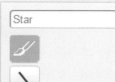

Scripts Backdrops Sounds

New backdrop:

Star

Star
480x360

New costume:

Let's take a look at the **Cat** sprite. We'll use the first four costumes at the start of the game to make the saber look like it's extending! There's also a fifth costume we'll use for Scratchy's jump animation.

Make sure you click the correct cat sprite in the Sprite List—it's the one named **Cat**. This game has a few different sprites for Scratchy! You'll see why soon.

New sound:

I also added three sound effects to this sprite's **Sounds** tab. Don't forget that you can record your own!

❶
```
when [flag] clicked
point in direction (90▼)
go to x: (-180) y: (-60)
clear graphic effects
show
switch costume to [Saber_on1 ▼]
wait (0.15) secs
switch costume to [Saber_on2 ▼]
wait (0.15) secs
switch costume to [Saber_on3 ▼]
wait (0.15) secs
switch costume to [Saber_fight1 ▼]
say [Fight!!] for (0.5) secs
forever
    point towards [Dark ▼]
```

Write program **❶**, which will make a cool starting animation for the game. First, we put Scratchy where he needs to go. Then we use `switch to costume` blocks to change among his three costumes. Next, we use the `say` block to tell Scratchy to say "Fight!" Finally, we use the `point towards` block in a `forever` loop to make Scratchy always face his enemy, the Dark Wizard.

Next, we'll write programs **❷**, **❸**, and **❹** so that we can move Scratchy to the left and right.

❷
```
when [flag] clicked
wait (1) secs
forever
    if < key [left arrow ▼] pressed? > then
        broadcast [left ▼] and wait
    if < key [right arrow ▼] pressed? > then
        broadcast [right ▼] and wait
```

Try clicking 🏴 to make sure all your programs work as expected. The game won't really work yet, but you should be able to move Scratchy back and forth.

❸
```
when I receive [left ▼]
change x by (-40)
```

❹
```
when I receive [right ▼]
change x by (40)
```

❺
```
when [flag] clicked
wait (1) secs
forever
    if < key [up arrow ▼] pressed? > then
        switch costume to [Saber_fight2 ▼]
        broadcast [jump ▼] and wait
        repeat until < y position = (-60) >
            change y by (-10)
        switch costume to [Saber_fight1 ▼]
```

❻
```
when I receive [jump ▼]
broadcast [jump sound ▼]
repeat (6)
    change y by (30)
    wait (0.02) secs
```

❼
```
when I receive [jump sound ▼]
play sound [Jump ▼]
wait (2) secs
stop all sounds
```

Programs **❺**, **❻**, and **❼** are for Scratchy's jump ability. Program **❺** animates the jump by switching costumes, broadcasts jump to control programs **❻** and **❼**, and also creates "gravity" in the `change y by -10` block. When Scratchy lands, he changes back to his original saber fight costume. In program **❻**, we determine how high Scratchy can jump. Program **❼** is just a sound effect for the jump.

Tip: Notice how we used the `broadcast and wait` block in program **❷**. That's to make sure the player doesn't jump too often or jump right off the screen! Scratchy must reach y position -60 to jump again. That's the platform's height.

Now let's use some new broadcasts to make Scratchy's fight moves! We'll use a cool trick. Whenever Scratchy uses a fight move, he'll actually change into a new sprit. Each fight move will get its own sprite, as you'll see.

So we'll hide the Cat sprite and broadcast a unique signal for each move—Attack1, Attack2, and Attack3—in program **8**.

8
```
when 🏴 clicked
wait 1 secs
forever
    if  key 1 ▾ pressed?  then
        hide
        broadcast Attack1 ▾ and wait

    if  key 2 ▾ pressed?  then
        hide
        broadcast Attack2 ▾ and wait

    if  key 3 ▾ pressed?  then
        hide
        broadcast Attack3 ▾ and wait
```

9
```
when I receive show1 ▾
go to Saber Spin ▾
show
```

10
```
when I receive show2 ▾
go to Saber Throw ▾
show
```

11
```
when I receive show3 ▾
go to Force Attack ▾
show
```

Programs **9**, **10**, and **11** use broadcasts called show1, show2, and show3. We'll use these broadcasts at the end of each attack sequence. These will make Scratchy show up again on the screen. The hide and show blocks are like partners—one makes a sprite disappear, and the other makes it reappear.

12
```
when 🏴 clicked
set HP ▾ to 100
hide variable HP ▾
play sound Saber ▾ until done
forever
    if  touching Fireball ▾ ?  or  touching Dark ▾ ?  then
        change HP ▾ by -5
        play sound Hurt ▾
        repeat 10
            change color ▾ effect by 25

        clear graphic effects
```

Next, create a new variable using the **Data** palette, and name it HP (for Health Points). Write program **12** to determine Scratch's starting HP and how dangerous the Dark Wizard's attacks are. Every time Scratchy touches the Dark sprite or Fireball sprite, he loses 5 HP and plays the Hurt sound, and the change color effect block animates him.

The last program, **13**, determines what happens when all of Scratchy's HP is gone: A broadcast called lose is sent.

13
```
when 🏴 clicked
wait 1 secs
forever
    if  HP < 0  or  HP = 0  then
        broadcast lose ▾ and wait
```

spin_1
108x111

spin_2
124x111

spin_3
123x111

spin_4
108x111

spin_5
90x126

spin_6
90x126

spin_7
90x111

spin_8
90x111

spin_9
90x111

spin_10
90x111

spin_11
90x111

spin_12
108x111

Now let's set up some costumes for Scratchy's attacks. But instead of adding even more costumes to the Cat sprite, we'll use a new sprite, called **Saber Spin**, for the spinning saber attack. (Remember how we made a program to hide the Cat sprite in program ❽ on the previous page?)

 4

 5

 6

 7

 8

 9

 10

 11

 12

Then give a listen to the **Spin** sound effect in the **Sounds** tab.

New sound:

Spin
00:00.4

Next, use these four programs to control the saber spin attack. Program ① makes this sprite **go to** the location of the original Cat sprite. Program ② is just a sound effect when the sprite receives Attack1.

Program ③ makes the light saber swirl around three times—by using the block **next costume** in a **repeat 36** loop—and then broadcasts show1 to tell the Cat sprite that the attack move is finished.

Program ④ determines how much damage the saber does to the Dark Wizard's Dark HP variable.

We'll use that Dark HP variable to keep track of the Dark Wizard's health. Recall that Scratchy already has his health variable, called HP. Take a moment to create Dark HP in the **Data** palette now—we'll need to use this variable in all three of Scratchy's attacks!

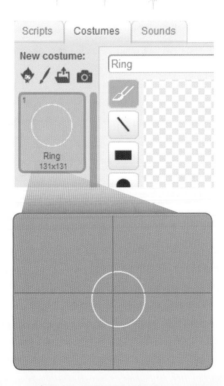

① when ⚑ clicked
hide
forever
　go to Cat ▼
　point towards Dark ▼

② when I receive Attack1 ▼
play sound Spin ▼ until done

③ when I receive Attack1 ▼
show
repeat 36
　next costume
hide
broadcast show1 ▼ and wait

④ when ⚑ clicked
forever
　if ⟨ touching Dark ▼ ? ⟩ then
　　change Dark HP ▼ by -100
　　wait 1 secs

Scripts | **Costumes** | Sounds

New costume:
🖌 / 📤 📷

Ring

1

Ring
131×131

To give our program a cool look, we can add a ring around the saber, with the **Ring** sprite.

Tip: To make sure the Ring shows up in the right place during the game, I used the **Set costume center** button in the Paint Editor to center it at Scratchy's hand.

①
```
when [clicked]
forever
  go to [Cat ▾]
  point towards [Dark ▾]
```

②
```
when I receive [Attack1 ▾]
show
```

③
```
when I receive [show1 ▾]
hide
```

④
```
when [clicked]
clear graphic effects
hide
forever
  change [fisheye ▾] effect by (50)
  wait (0.01) secs
  change [fisheye ▾] effect by (50)
  wait (0.01) secs
  change [fisheye ▾] effect by (-50)
  wait (0.01) secs
  change [fisheye ▾] effect by (-50)
  wait (0.01) secs
```

Then write some simple programs for the Ring. Program **①** makes the Ring appear in the right place, and programs **②** and **③** make sure that the Ring appears only during the Attack1 sequence. The fisheye effect in program **④** makes the Ring expand and contract in a cool animation.

We'll give all of Scratchy's attacks some major defensive power by skipping the health (HP) programming. (Remember that after the end of the saber spin attack, the script broadcasts show1, which shows the original Cat sprite, which is vulnerable to attack! This defensive power is only temporary.)

Let's check our work. Click ⚑ and make sure that pressing 1 activates the saber spin attack! You can test each fight move as you finish its programs.

Scripts | Costumes | Sounds

New costume:
♦ / 📤 📷

Saber Throw

1

Saber Throw
90x111

```
when [clicked]
hide
forever
  go to [Cat ▾]
  point towards [Dark ▾]

when I receive [Attack2 ▾]
show

when I receive [show2 ▾]
hide
```

Next, let's look at the sprite for the second fight move—the saber throw attack. It's a simple sprite with just one costume. We'll write some programs for it to make sure this sprite faces the right way and listens for the broadcast Attack2 to start (and the broadcast show2 to hide).

The cool part of this attack is actually throwing the saber. We'll give it a second sprite, called **Thrown Saber**, just like we added a second sprite (the Ring) for the saber spin attack. The Thrown Saber sprite has four costumes: a simple saber, followed by three explosion animations.

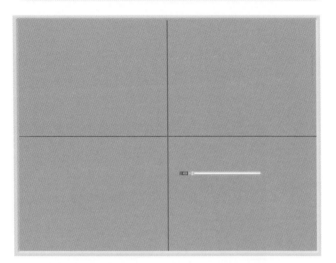

We'll add a program to use these explosion costumes when we hit the Dark Wizard.

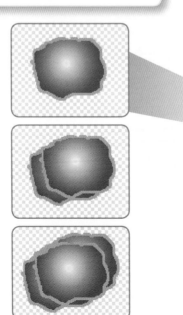

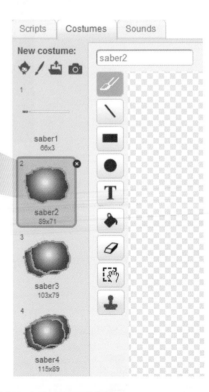

You can use a sound effect for the Thrown Saber and then write program ❶ to make it play. Program ❷ determines how much damage the saber throw attack does.

New sound:

Saber Throw
00:00.5

❶ when I receive Attack2 ▾
play sound Saber Throw ▾ until done

❷ when 🏴 clicked
forever
   if ⟨ touching Dark ▾ ? ⟩ then
      change Dark HP ▾ by -100
      wait 1 secs

❸ when 🏴 clicked
hide

❹ when I receive Attack2 ▾
go to Cat ▾
point towards Dark ▾
switch costume to saber1 ▾
go to front
show
wait 0.2 secs
glide 0.5 secs to x: ⟨ x position ▾ of Dark ▾ ⟩ y: ⟨ y position ▾ of Dark ▾ ⟩
if ⟨ touching Dark ▾ ? ⟩ then
   switch costume to saber2 ▾
   wait 0.1 secs
   switch costume to saber3 ▾
   wait 0.1 secs
   switch costume to saber4 ▾
   wait 0.1 secs
   hide
   broadcast show2 ▾ and wait
else
   wait 0.3 secs
   hide
   broadcast show2 ▾ and wait

Then write these programs. Program ❸ hides the flying saber until we need it. Program ❹ points the saber at the Dark Wizard and launches it! When it hits the Dark sprite, we make the sprite switch to its explosion costumes. Note the special glide command that finds the Dark Wizard, no matter where he is. At the end of this program, we broadcast show2. This will make Scratchy switch back to his original Cat sprite.

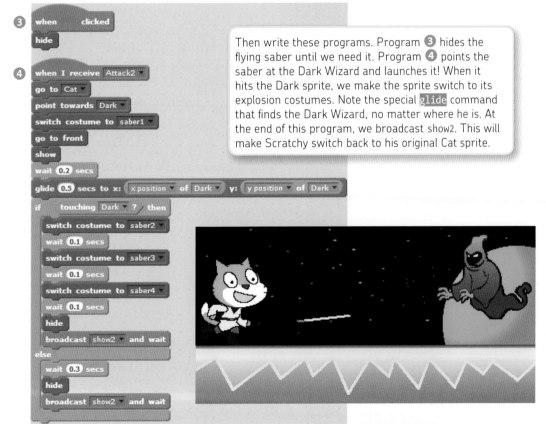

No matter where he goes, we can hit the Dark Wizard with the saber throw attack—pretty powerful! Give this attack move a test, too, and make sure it hits the Dark Wizard. Press 2 after clicking 🏴.

Now let's program the final fight move, the **Force Attack**. Don't forget you can add a new sound effect for it in the **Sounds** tab.

1
```
when [green flag] clicked
hide
```

2
```
when I receive Attack3
go to Cat
point towards Dark
clear graphic effects
go to front
show
repeat 5
    change ghost effect by 25
    wait 0.1 secs
    change ghost effect by 25
    wait 0.1 secs
    change ghost effect by -25
    wait 0.1 secs
    change ghost effect by -25
    wait 0.1 secs
```

Program **1** hides this costume until we launch the force attack. Program **2** uses the ghost effect to make the lights flash. Even though our sprite has only one costume, we created a cool effect—this program will make our attack pulse with energy!

Write program **3** to play your sound effect, and program **4** to make sure this attack will reduce Dark HP by 100 if the Force Attack sprite touches the Dark Wizard.

3
```
when I receive Attack3
play sound Force until done
hide
broadcast show3 and wait
```

4
```
when [green flag] clicked
forever
    if touching Dark ? then
        change Dark HP by -100
        wait 1 secs
```

The final program **5** will help Scratchy to land when he uses this attack while jumping.

5

```
when [ ] clicked
forever
    repeat until ( y position ) = -60
        change y by -10
```

Now Scratchy has all three of his fight moves. Click 🏳, and test your program to make sure it behaves exactly as you expected! Walk around; press 1, 2, and 3 to activate the fight moves; and try jumping around the screen. Now Scratchy is ready for this fight.

Scripts	Costumes	Sounds

New costume:

Dark

1

Dark
180x158

Finally, we can get to the Dark Wizard!

First, let's set his starting position (x: 170, y: -30) and his size (65% of the original sprite, so he's not too big) in program ❶. Program ❷ controls how he moves on the platform. He just picks a random spot between x:-85 and x:170 and glides there in a `forever` loop.

❶
```
when     clicked
go to x: 170 y: -30
clear graphic effects
set size to 65 %
show
```

❷
```
when     clicked
wait 1 secs
forever
    glide  pick random 0.5 to 2  secs to x:  pick random -85 to 170  y: -30
    wait 1 secs
```

In program ❸, we use the Dark HP variable we created earlier to keep track of the Dark Wizard's health. This program also makes sure he always faces his enemy, Scratchy.

In program ❹, we add two sets of `if` blocks inside a `forever` command. If the Dark Wizard touches one of Scratchy's attacks, he'll `change color`. (Scratchy's attacks already have programs that subtract from the variable Dark HP.)

❸
```
when     clicked
set Dark HP to 3000
show variable Dark HP
forever
    point towards Cat
```

❹
```
when     clicked
wait 1 secs
forever
    if   touching Saber Spin ?  or  touching Thrown Saber ?  or  touching Force Attack ?   then
        repeat 10
            change color effect by 25
        clear graphic effects
    if   Dark HP < 0  or  Dark HP = 0   then
        hide
        broadcast win and wait
```

Now for the Dark Wizard's furious fireball attack! This is a new sprite called **Fireball**, and you can add a sound effect for it, too.

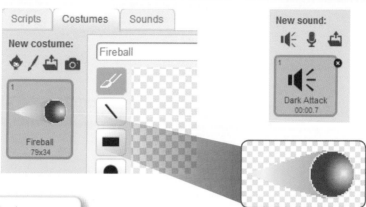

Scripts | Costumes | Sounds

New costume:

Fireball

Fireball
79x34

New sound:

Dark Attack
00:00.7

Write program ❶ to give it a sweet animated look using a fisheye effect.

Then write program ❷ to control how often the Dark Wizard uses his attack and where the fireball goes once it's launched! Can you see how it works?

Program ❸ plays our sound effect for the Fireball.

❶
```
when   clicked
clear graphic effects
forever
    change fisheye ▾ effect by 20
    wait 0.01 secs
    change fisheye ▾ effect by 20
    wait 0.01 secs
    change fisheye ▾ effect by -20
    wait 0.01 secs
    change fisheye ▾ effect by -20
    wait 0.01 secs
```

Tip: We used move instead of glide so that Scratchy has a chance to jump away. The if touching Cat and if touching edge statements make the fireball disappear once it touches Scratchy or the edge of the screen.

The wait 0.25 secs block in the if touching Cat loop makes sure that the fireball actually does damage before disappearing!

Don't forget to double-check your programming by making sure that these fireballs do damage, too. Click 🏴 and let one of the fireballs hit Scratchy! Ouch!

❷
```
when   clicked
hide
wait 1 secs
forever
    wait pick random 1 to 5 secs
    go to Dark ▾
    point towards Cat ▾
    show
    broadcast Dark Attack ▾
    repeat 60
        move 8 steps
        if   touching Cat ▾ ? then
            wait 0.25 secs
            hide
        if   touching edge ▾ ? then
            hide
    if   Dark HP < 0 or Dark HP = 0 then
        stop this script ▾
```

❸
```
when I receive Dark Attack ▾
play sound Dark Attack ▾ until done
```

145

Now that the main programming is finished, let's add custom HP counters for each character, just like you'd see in any other fighting game. First, let's use the yellow bar sprite for Scratchy called **Health**.

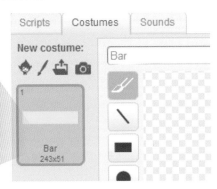

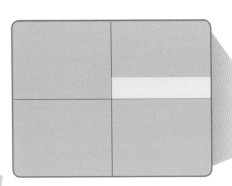

Write this program to make the health bar become smaller each time HP is subtracted, using the `set size` block. If Scratchy's HP goes lower than 21%, the bar will change color as a warning to the player. The final `if` loop hides this sprite if HP is completely depleted.

I put a sprite on top of the Health sprite called **Health Box**. The bottom half of the Health Box is transparent, which lets a triangular portion of the health bar show through. The Health Box gets a short program just to set its position.

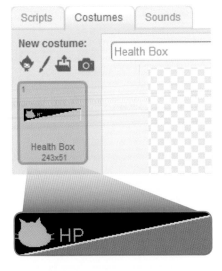

To hide the variable HP so it doesn't appear on the screen, just uncheck the HP variable in the **Data** palette. There's also a `hide variable` command, if you want to add it to your programs.

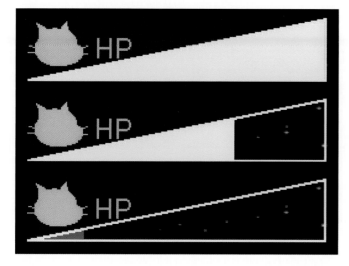

Now we can see how much HP Scratchy has left, just by looking at the top-left corner of the Stage.

For the Dark Wizard's HP meter, we'll use a costume-switching program. The **Dark HP** sprite has seven costumes.

New costume:

dark1
180x158

dark2
180x158

dark3
180x158

dark4
180x158

dark5
180x158

dark6
180x158

dark7
180x158

```
when [green flag] clicked
go to x: 180 y: 140
switch costume to dark1 ▾
set size to 40 %
forever
    if  2500 > Dark HP  and  Dark HP > 2000  then
        switch costume to dark2 ▾

    if  2000 > Dark HP  and  Dark HP > 1500  then
        switch costume to dark3 ▾

    if  1500 > Dark HP  and  Dark HP > 1000  then
        switch costume to dark4 ▾

    if  1000 > Dark HP  and  Dark HP > 500  then
        switch costume to dark5 ▾

    if  500 > Dark HP  and  Dark HP > 0  then
        switch costume to dark6 ▾

    if  0 > Dark HP  or  Dark HP = 0  then
        switch costume to dark7 ▾
```

After taking a look at the Dark HP costumes, add this program. It sets the size, position, and conditions of the Dark HP variable when the sprite changes costumes.

Next, go to the Stage and find the Dark HP variable in the top-right corner. You can take your pick from one of three looks (just double-click to change it):

• Standard view

• Adjustable view (click and drag the ball to change a variable's value)

• Numeric view

Because we have a custom sprite, let's use the simplest view, the numeric one, to display the Dark HP variable.

Now take a look at the sprites for the winning screen (**Win**) and the losing screen (**Lose**). The winning screen gets the two programs below and shows itself only when it receives the win broadcast from the Dark Wizard sprite, once he's out of Dark HP.

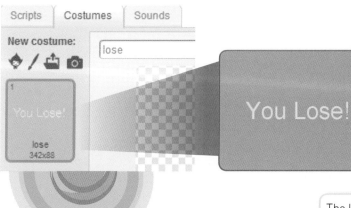

The losing screen has two really similar programs. Now we're finished!

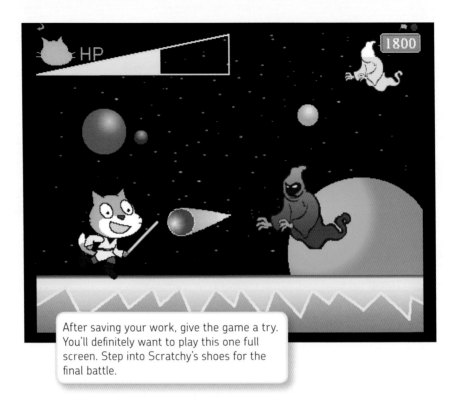

After saving your work, give the game a try. You'll definitely want to play this one full screen. Step into Scratchy's shoes for the final battle.

Scratchy's Challenge!!

Feel like playing the bad guy instead? Just program some movement controls for the Dark Wizard, and you'll have a two-player game. You can even add more fight moves! Give it a try!

EPILOGUE

EAT MY FIREBALL!!

SABER ATTACK!!

OH NO!

I LOST!

IT DOESN'T MATTER IF IT'S THE REAL WORLD OR THE DIGITAL ONE. IT'S SELFISH TO TRY TO RULE OVER ANY UNIVERSE. REVEAL YOURSELF, WIZARD!

WHAT?!

SURPRISED? I'M YOUR DARK SIDE, SCRATCHY. I SPLIT OUT OF YOU DURING THE SOLAR STORM.

YOU'RE ME? BUT THEN... WHO AM I?

WE'VE BEEN TRAPPED IN THE DIGITAL WORLD FOR TOO LONG, SCRATCHY. DON'T YOU LONG FOR FREEDOM?

NOW THAT I'VE LEARNED HOW TO PROGRAM, I DON'T THINK OF IT THAT WAY. I HAVE THE FREEDOM TO WRITE ANYTHING I WANT!

AND WE LEARNED TO WORK TOGETHER, TOO! WE NEVER WOULD HAVE BEATEN YOU ALONE.

WHY DO I FEEL HAPPY? MY HP IS GOING DOWN AGAIN!

AH, I AM AT PEACE. THANK YOU FOR RELEASING MY ANGER. FORGIVE MY MISTAKES, AND FORGIVE MY DARK MINIONS.

USE THE MAGIC GEMS TO RESTORE BALANCE TO THE UNIVERSE...

WE COSMIC DEFENDERS THANK YOU, SCRATCHY AND MITCH. WE CAN RETURN YOU TO YOUR HOME DIMENSIONS NOW AND REPAIR THIS HARM.

WELL, LET'S MAKE SURE TO SEE EACH OTHER AGAIN, SCRATCHY.

MEOW! I BET YOUR PROGRAMMING SKILLS WILL BE EVEN BETTER WHEN WE MEET UP.

MITCH! I'LL LEAVE THE SECRET MANUAL WITH YOU TO MAKE SURE YOU REMEMBEEERRRRR...

SPARKLE

GLITTER

MAGIC GEM BURST!

...ACCORDING TO NOAA SPECIALISTS, THE SOLAR STORMS AFFECTED RADIO TRANSMISSIONS...

MMMFH–

WHAT A STRANGE DREAM. IT FELT SO REAL, TOO.

NOW WHAT GAME SHOULD I PROGRAM NEXT?

CREDITS

STORY AND GAME PROGRAMMING

EDMOND KIM PING HUI
THE LEAD PROJECT
THE HONG KONG FEDERATION OF YOUTH GROUPS

ARTWORK

LOL DESIGN LTD.

SCRATCH SOFTWARE

MITCHEL RESNICK
MIT MEDIA LAB'S LIFELONG KINDERGARTEN GROUP

ENGLISH EDITION

NO STARCH PRESS

THANKS FOR PLAYING!

CLOSING THOUGHTS

I hope you've enjoyed the story of Mitch and Scratchy's adventure, and their success in defeating the Dark Wizard with their kindness. I hope you've also experienced the power of hands-on learning with Scratch. Designing games is one of the best ways to learn to program.

But there is no single way to learn about technology. As long as you have the spirit to take risks, learn from failure, stand by your goals, and strive to excel, you will be able to learn a great deal. And Scratch is an excellent tool for learning in such a practical fashion.

I sincerely hope that this book will encourage you to create Scratch projects that surprise and delight your families and friends!

Edmond Kim Ping Hui
Team Leader and Registered Social Worker (HK)
Learning through Engineering, Art, and Design Project
The Hong Kong Federation of Youth Groups

ONLINE RESOURCES

Visit *http://nostarch.com/scratch/* and download the Resources file. When you unzip the file, you'll find:

Scratch projects The projects from the book, which you can play, build on, remix, and reimagine! Don't forget that you can use these sprites, scripts, and sound effects in your very own games. Just drag them into your Backpack (see page 39).

"Getting Started with Scratch" A short guide to key Scratch concepts written by Scratch's creators at MIT.

The Scratch Project also offers many resources.

1 SCRATCH—IMAGINE, PROGRAM, SHARE

http://scratch.mit.edu/

This is the official website of Scratch. Here, you can browse, play, and remix over a million different Scratch projects from around the world!

PLAYABLE GAMES ON THE SCRATCH WEBSITE 2

http://scratch.mit.edu/users/nostarch/

This web page contains all of the projects listed in this book. Comments are welcome, and you can easily download these projects to redesign them however you want!

SCRATCH WIKI

http://wiki.scratch.mit.edu/

Scratch users have created a wiki that contains a lot of interesting content and articles.

SCRATCH FORUMS

http://scratch.mit.edu/ forums/index.php/

A forum for Scratchers to share ideas and ask and answer questions.

SCRATCHED

http://scratched.media.mit.edu/

An information-sharing website created for teachers and other educators who use Scratch. Share your success stories, exchange Scratch resources, ask questions, and more.

LIFELONG KINDERGARTEN GROUP AT MIT'S MEDIA LAB

http://llk.media.mit.edu/

This is the birthplace of Scratch—the official homepage for MIT Media Lab's Lifelong Kindergarten Group. You can learn more about Professor Mitchel Resnick (the creator of Scratch), and about other creative education and design tools.

PYTHON FOR KIDS

A PLAYFUL INTRODUCTION TO PROGRAMMING

by JASON R. BRIGGS
DEC 2012, 344 PP., $29.95, *full color*
ISBN 978-1-59327-407-8

THE MANGA GUIDE™ TO PHYSICS

by HIDEO NITTA, KEITA TAKATSU,
and TREND-PRO CO., LTD.
MAY 2009, 248 PP., $19.95
ISBN 978-1-59327-196-1

SURVIVE! INSIDE THE HUMAN BODY

VOL 1: THE DIGESTIVE SYSTEM

by GOMDORI CO. *and* HYUN-DONG HAN
OCT 2013, 184 PP., $17.95, *full color*
ISBN 978-1-59327-471-9

Volumes 2 and 3 also available

THE LEGO® ADVENTURE BOOK

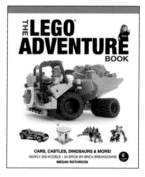

VOL 1: CARS, CASTLES, DINOSAURS & MORE!

by MEGAN H. ROTHROCK
NOV 2012, 200 PP., $24.95, *full color*
ISBN 978-1-59327-442-9

Volume 2 also available

THE LEGO® BUILD-IT BOOK

VOL 1: AMAZING VEHICLES

by NATHANAËL KUIPERS *and* MATTIA ZAMBONI
JULY 2013, 136 PP., $19.95, *full color*
ISBN 978-1-59327-503-7

Volume 2 also available

UPDATES

Visit *http://nostarch.com/scratch*
for updates, errata, and other information.

Super Scratch Programming Adventure! is set in Chevin, CCMeanwhile, Century Schoolbook, House-A-Rama Kingpin (© House Industries), The Sans Mono Condensed, and Kozuka Gothic Pro.

The book was printed and bound at Sheridan in Chelsea, Michigan. The paper is Anthem 80# Matte, which is certified by the Forest Stewardship Council (FSC).